To William A. Morowitz, M.D.
Pulmonologist

A literary and photographic gift
in appreciation for your understanding
of test results of this poetic patient.
Your insight into techniques and
procedures to be followed after
my diagnosis with macroglobulinemia
avoided unnecessary biopsies and
helped ensure remission. Your
skills and decision-making helped
make this collection of poems and
photographs a reality.

Best wishes for reading and
viewing enjoyment.

Craig E. Burgess

A Fleeting Glimpse of Paradise

Photographic and Poetic Images of the Hawaiian Islands

by

Craig E. Burgess

DORRANCE PUBLISHING CO
EST. 1920
PITTSBURGH, PENNSYLVANIA 15238

Photography by Craig E. Burgess.
Color maps courtesy of *This Week Magazine:* William Buddy Moore, Senior Director of Operations.

Dorrance Publishing Co
585 Alpha Drive
Suite 103
Pittsburgh, PA 15238
Visit our website at *www.dorrancebookstore.com*

ISBN: 978-1-4809-2034-7
eISBN: 978-1-4809-2149-8

A Fleeting Glimpse of Paradise is dedicated to all of the local residents on the islands of Hawaii who have made me part of their "ohana" and who have shared the spirit of Aloha with me as I learned more about the history and about the culture of the Hawaiian people.

Without the support of these residents, this tribute in verse and photography would never have been completed.

Mahalo nui loa!

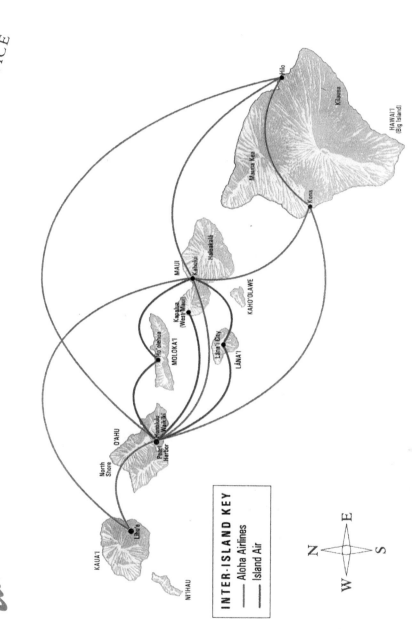

Aloha Airlines & Island Air
INTER-ISLAND SERVICE

INTER-ISLAND KEY
—— Aloha Airlines
—— Island Air

KAUA'I
Līhu'e
NI'IHAU
O'AHU
North Shore
Honolulu
Wai'Ki
Pearl Harbor
MOLOKA'I
Ho'olehua
LĀNA'I
Lāna'i City
MAUI
Kapalua (West Maui)
Kahului
Haleakalā
KAHO'OLAWE
HAWAI'I (Big Island)
Mauna Kea
Kīlauea
Hilo
Kona

N
E
S
W

Acknowledgments

A. General

Audubon Jr. and Sr. High School, Audubon, New Jersey
    Project Memorial Foundation Committee
    Mr. John Skrabonja, English and Guidance Departments (p. 338)
    Mr. Brian Kulak, English Department (p. 338)
    Miss Tara Conte, AHS Class of 2003 (pp. 334, 338)

Ritz Camera at Echelon Mall, Voorhees, New Jersey
    Mr. Ken Wolf, Manager
    Mr. John Headley
    Ms. Andrea Bird
    Ms. Virginia Densten
    Mr. Ben Riley
    Mr. Jason Hall

Cherry Hill High School EAST, Cherry Hill, New Jersey
    Ms. Sara Jane Carmody, English Department
    Mr. John Skrabonja Jr., CHHSE Class of 2003
    CHHSE Adopt-A-Grandparent Program
    CHHSE Passport International Language Magazine

Commercial Printing in Wenatchee, Washington
    Mr. Michael C. Terrell, Owner
    Mr. Tom Wentz

The Department of the U.S. Navy (pp. 39-42)

Redrosebush Press, Wenatchee, Washington
Mrs. Ella M. Dillon, Publisher

Fujifilm Corporation
> All of the photos taken by the author for this collection were shot with
> QUICKSNAP Flash 35-mm One-Time-Use Cameras using Fuji film

Pearl Harbor Survivors' Club in San Diego, California
> Mr. Gordon Jones, President

Office Max at Lion's Head Plaza in Somerdale, New Jersey
> Ms. Debbie Jones, Branch Manager
> Ms. Sandra Benson, CopyMax Supervisor
> Ms. Tanya Mendoza
> Ms. Kelly Nueman

B. Introduction

Bubba Gump Restaurant & Market, Lahaina, Maui (pp. xvii, 170, 171, 376)
> Ms. Cathy Peterson, Head of Marketing, San Clemente, California
> Mr. Ken Allen, Manager
> Mr. Sean O'Donnell, Assistant Manager

Aloha International (p. xxxiv)
> Dr. Serge King, Executive Director
> Peggy Kemp, Administrator

C. Cruising on the SS *Independence*

American Hawaii Cruise Lines (pp. xxxvi-26, 28)
> Mr. Kamana'o Hattori, Cruise Director (pp. 1, 3-4)
> Kumu Haunani Kaui (pp.5-7, 132-135, 153)
> Kumu Kahea Beckley (pp. 7, 152-153)
> Mr. Butch O'Sullivan, Entertainer (pp. 8-13)
> Kawika Kaui (pp. 14-17, 134-136)

Monta Vista High School, Cupertino, California (p. 18)
Student Group, The Impressions
Na Hula O Kaohikukapulani,
Kumu Kapu Kinimaka Alquiza, Teacher (p. 22)

D. Oahu

Pleasant Hawaii, Publication of *This Week Magazine* (pp. 27, 61, 141, 165)
William Buddy Moore, Senior Director of Operations, *This Week Publications*, Honolulu, Hawaii
Administrators of the USS *Arizona* Memorial (pp. 31-38)
Outrigger Beach Hotel, Waikiki Beach (pp. 47-49)
The Royal Hawaiian Hotel, Waikiki Beach (pp. 50-53)
Dole Pineapple Plantation (p. 55)
Turtle Bay Resort on North Shore (pp. 57-58)
Debbie Miles, Public Relations
Polynesian Cultural Center (pp. 59-60)

E. Kauai

State Parks of Kauai
Waimea High School, Waimea (pp. 65, 69-73)
Vice Principal Cabuto
Borders Books & Music, Lihue (pp. 69, 74-75)
Tiffany C. R. Woodard, Manager
Mr. Shannon Hart, English Department, Waimea H. S. (pp. 65-67, 70)
Mrs. Mary Daubert, Current Marketing Manager for the Kukui Grove Center; former C. R. C. for Borders in Lihue (pp. 64, 73-75)
The Green Garden Restaurant, Hanapepe (pp. 76-77)
The Kaui Family: Wesley, Trinette, Donovan (Kale), David (Kawika) (pp. 81, 89-96, 133, 136)
The Kilohana Plantation (pp. 97-99, 139)
Mr. Tony Martin, Plantation Carriage Driver
Wailua State Park and Fern Grotto (pp. 103-105)
Ms. Caroline Guerrero, Manager, Waialeale Tours
Kilauea Lighthouse (pp. 110-113)
Mr. Dave Aplin, State Park Contact

Princeville Resort and Hotel Complex (pp. 115-116)
        Auntie Louise Marston, Hanalei (pp. 118-120)
Inter-Island Helicopters (pp. 121-124)
Blue Dolphin Cruises (pp. 126-127)
Radisson Kauai Beach Resort (pp. 128-130)
        Mr. Tom Bartlett, Manager
        Mr. Glenn T. Ichimura, Painter
Kauai Hula Girl Restaurant, Kapaa (pp. 134-135)
        Ms. Keala Kinimaka Senkus, Hula Kumu

F. Hawaii

Hale Aloha Nazarene School, Hilo (pp. 142, 146)
        Mrs. Endriss, Teacher
Volcanoes' National Park Staff (pp. 149-150)
Hawaiian Paradise Trading Co.
        James Raschick, President
        Mr. Herbert Kane, Artist, Historian (p. 151)
Hawaii National Parks Administration (pp. 154-160)
Parker Ranch Riding School (pp. 161-164)
        Ms. Karoll Penovaroff, Owner

G. Maui

Papakea Resort, Honokō wai (p. 169)
Maui Ocean Center, Maalaea (pp. 178-183)
        Ms. Liz Warrick, Public Relations Manager
Maui Tropical Plantation (pp. 184-185)
        Mr. Reny Platz, Manager
Iao Valley Park Staff (pp. 186-187)
Baldwin High School, Wailuku (pp. 189-199)
        Principal Yamada
        Vice Principal McClelland
        Mr. Wallace Kuloloio (pp. 193-194)
        Ms. Janet Sato, Art Instructor (p, 195)
        CSM Peter Pacyao, JROTC (pp. 196-199)
Maui Arts & Cultural Center, Kahului (pp. 200-212)

Ms. Christina Cowan, President and CEO

Mr. Keali'i Reichel, Singer / Songwriter (pp. 202-210)

Punahele Productions,

Mr. Fred Krauss, President

Ku'ulei Martinson, Quilter (pp. 211-212)

Hawaii Video Memories

Nichol Nagata (pp. 213-219)

Ekahi Tours (pp. 220-222)

Borders Books & Music, Kahului (pp. 223-225)

Starscape Music (pp. 223-225)

Nona and Keola Beamer

Doris Todd Memorial Christian School, Paia (pp. 226-231)

Principal Jan Fuller

Mama's Fish House, Kuau Cove (Front Cover, Back Cover; pp. 232-240, 242)

Mr. Floyd Christienson, Owner

Mr. Martin Lenny, General Manager (Until March, 2003)

Mr. Kevin O'Malley, Assistant Manager

Mr. Dennis Daly, Host

Ms. Joanne Lukin, Hostess

Mrs. Diana Stuart (pp. 238-239, 243-245)

Old Lahaina Luau (p. 245)

Mr. Michael Moore, General Manager

The Thompson Ranch (p. 254)

Haleakala National Park (pp. 255-261)

The Kihei Canoe Club, Ka Lae Pohaku Beach (pp. 266-279)

Mr. Maile Arensdorf, President

Mr. Alika Atay, Past-President

Mr. Tevita Lotoaatu, Master Carver

61 S. Kihei Road (pp. 280-282)

Mr. Jesse Nakooka, "Mr. Maui" (pp. 283-286)

Trinity Episcopal Church-By-The-Sea, Kihei (pp. 287-292)

The Reverend Morley E. Frech, Rector

Mrs. Ruth Murata-Eisen, Organist

Mrs. Cora Camarillo, Hula Performer

The Maui Schooner Resort, Kihei (pp. 294-305)

Mrs. Nancy Geist, General Manager

Mr. David Geist, Landscaper

The Diamond Resort, Wailea (pp. 310-313)

Kyoko Kimura, General Manager

The Maui Island Weekly (p. 314)

        Mr. Joseph Sugarman, Reporter

        Mr. Tony Van Steen, Tennis Instructor / Pianist (pp. 314-325)

The SeaWatch Restaurant at Wailea (pp. 326-330)

        Ms. Gerri Eckart, Manager

        Mrs. Skipper Smith, Dance Instructor (pp. 329-331)

The Maui Writers' Conference (pp. 333-338)

        Mr. John Tullius, Founder (p. 337)

        Mrs. Shannon Tullius, Founder of the Young Writers' Program (p. 337)

        Ms. Sam Horn, Author, Speaker, Hostess of the Annual Conference (p. 337)

        Mr. Jack Canfield, Author / Motivational Speaker (p. 334)

H. Patriotism in the Fiftieth State

KPOA Radio, 93.5 FM (p. 353)

        Ms. Alakai Paleka, Program Director and "Morning Goddess"

The Maui News (p. 354)

        Mr. David Hoff, Editor-in-Chief

        Ms. Claudine San Nicolas, Reporter

        Mr. Albert Franco, World War II Navy Veteran (pp. 355-358)

The Maui Weekly (pp. 355, 357)

        Ms. Kathy Helmick, Office Manager

I. Conclusion

The Los Angeles Times (p.368)

        Mr. Gary Polakovic, Reporter

Foreword

The collection of poetry and photographs you are about to experience reflects my love for the islands of Hawaii: the beauty of the landscapes; the awe of special encounters; my gratitude to local residents who, sensing I had come for more than just a luau, a hula show, and a colorful Hawaiian shirt, willingly shared their experiences with me. The conversations with young students, musicians, artists, teachers (kumus), and longtime local residents provided the inspiration for this book.

May my thoughts and photographic images inspire *YOU* to learn more about America's fiftieth state and to reflect in your own lives—in the coming years—the SPIRIT OF ALOHA of the Hawaiian people.

Outrigger canoes on the Kihei Canoe Club Beach in Kihei, Maui

Scenic beauty of Kuau Cove and Mama's Fish House on Maui

Contents

An Introduction to the Experience: Some Opening Images xvii

Cruising on the SS *Independence* 1

Oahu 30

Kauai 63

Hawaii 142

Maui 166

Patriotism in the Fiftieth State 345

Conclusion 361

About the Author 377

An Introduction to the Experience:
Some Opening Images

*I*n putting together this collection, I first had to work on the presentation of material. How could I best create for you, the reader, a sense of excitement and adventure as I open your eyes and mind to the beauty of the islands? Perhaps a visual image would be a good start, showing me waiting, as a typical "tourist", for my first tour of the Island of Maui, back in 1974....

Author Burgess at Bubba Gump's, Lahaina, Maui

Ready to Begin

I wish I could tell you
The emotions that I feel,
Sitting on this special bench;
It almost seems unreal...
From the Kahului Airport
On Maui, the Valley Isle,
I traveled by coach through cane fields
To Lahaina, never losing my smile.
The West Maui Mountains are awesome;
The beaches—caressed by the hands
Of emerald-colored waters—
Sparkle more like diamonds than sands.
An afternoon shower produces
A huge double rainbow so bright
That I feel that the coach is taking me
To hidden treasures, still out of sight.

Be my guest, hop on board, and come with me!
We can share some adventures unique
While observing THE SPIRIT OF ALOHA
On the islands of Hawaii this week.

When I first came to Hawaii, back in 1973, I had only flown once: with a college roommate to Jamaica. Back in the 1970s, all major airlines flew into Honolulu on the island of Oahu. From there, any visits to other islands (Hawaii, Kauai, Maui) were possible only by small island commuter planes (Aloha and Hawaiian Air). Each "tourist" encountered—and still does in 2004—the unexpected surprises associated with...

The Challenge of Open Seating

When commuting on the airlines
Through the Hawaiian Island chain,
One receives NO seat assignment—
Which drives many tourists insane!

Most visitors want to be first in line
For a twenty-five minute flight,
So a line begins forming quickly...
BEFORE the plane is in sight!

Passengers stand in this extended "Q"
For thirty-five minutes or more.
Taking advantage of "open seating"—
Trying to get to row four.

Just "hang loose", Hawaiian traveler:
Enjoy this part of your stay.
MAHALO for being courteous
And, as always, have a great day!

At least back then, part of the fun of traveling was the opportunity to converse with fellow passengers. Ah, yes... "the good ole days". As we enter the twenty-first century—even when going on vacation!—modern technology tags along: an absolute must for survival! (?) Having traveled more than six hundred thousand miles in the past fifteen years (trips that include forty-one visits to Hawaii from the state of New Jersey), I have witnessed, first hand...

The Changing World of Travel

In our wondrous new age of technology,
There is never a second to lose.
Travelers now take their work with them,
Whether flying, or just on a cruise.
Airlines have lounges at airports
So that businessmen will not lose much time
Keeping in touch with their clients
As the corporate ladder they climb.

Most planes now have phones in the seatbacks,
Which are accessed by most credit cards,
So that passengers may set up appointments...
Or check on their pets in their yards.

And NOW there are laptop computers,
So compact they fit under your seat.
Thus, while in the air, you can finish
A proposal that is structured and neat,
Then FAX it to a number of colleagues
To get feedback before you arrive
At the site of the next business meeting—
So your "team" toward excellence may strive.

There's no time to talk with the person
Who sits at your side on the flight...
And so, he or she sits in silence:
To talk would not be polite.

"This is some introduction, Mr. Burgess. As the reader, I certainly hope the image you are creating will quickly become more positive in nature!"

Not to worry, dear reader. I felt it was necessary to put a little "reality" into my experience. However, remember that I have traveled five thousand miles from my home to visit Hawaii on forty-one occasions—and the best is now awaiting...

Once on the islands, it doesn't take long before the beauty of the islands begins to penetrate all of your senses. Perhaps, after a good night's sleep, you will awaken early, go for a walk, and experience...

The Joys of Early Morning

I watch as the sun ushers in a new day,
Then follow the butterflies in brilliant display,
Overhear conversations of birds in the palms,
Sense the joy of all Nature as it soothes and it calms,
Feel the touch of the breeze as it softly wafts by,
Smell the fragrance of flowers, which the breeze lifts on high,
Touch the droplets of dew on the glistening grass,
Spot some playful crustaceans on the beach as I pass,
See the algae afloat on the incoming tide,
Speak to seagulls and pelicans as on updrafts they glide,
Reach up to the heavens and silently pray,
Then rejoice as a witness to Nature's display…
For I'm blessed with the senses through which I explore
All of Nature's great beauty—and expressions galore—
As I walk and observe, to my mind's great delight,
What most take for granted in the dawn's early light.

As you observe more and more, you may be one of the fortunate visitors who becomes more aware of…

Kuau Cove, Maui

Carved wooden sea turtle waits to greet visitors at Club Lanai

The True Beauty of Hawaii

When most people think of Hawaii,
Those islands of Paradise,
They think of palm trees and waterfalls,
Of flower leis, of luaus, and of rice.
They want to "experience" the islands
On a tour that allows them to see
All the physical beauty of the landscape:
In adventures, both on land and at sea.

Very few visitors, however,
Observe the TRUE beauty that's there.
They spend their time running from place to place,
Forgetting some "Aloha" to share.
They ignore making contact with residents;
They abuse what the landscape provides.
For them, it's a nice place to visit…
Not a home in which a culture resides.

Should YOU ever decide to vacation
On one of the isles of Hawaii,
Take time to talk with the people
On Oahu, on Maui, on Kauai.
Show some respect for the landscape
As you plan, day by day, what to see.
Only then will you truly discover
How rewarding your vacation will be.

An island sport that is very popular is windsurfing. As the Tradewinds increase in the afternoon, you will encounter hundreds of special athletes, testing their skills against the elements. Let's take a closer look at a day in the life of…

The Windsurfer

Part I: The Preparation

On the grass near the beach in Kuau
The windsurfer kneels by his board.
He carefully checks his equipment:
The surfboard, the sail, every cord.
He knows that this step is important
To success, and he takes lots of time
Checking, then testing each item,
Before on the board he does climb.

Part II: The Technique

The strength of this athlete shows clearly—
And his knowledge of wind and tide times—
As he carries his board through the breakers,
Then onto the board deftly climbs.
He always maintains perfect balance
As he walks down the beach through the waves!
I'm amazed at how quickly he does it...
And of course, lots of energy saves
For the task that demands his attention,
His strength, his desire, his skill:
The conquest of dear Mother Nature
Whose powers will challenge his will
To ride o'er the waves like a feather—
First outward and then back to shore—
Displaying his incredible talent...
Then awaiting the judges' next score!

Part III: The Ride

Let's hop on the windsurfer's surfboard
Waterproof cam'ra in hand.
And go on a mem'rable journey
Far removed from the palm trees and sand.

Be careful! And don't lose your balance
As the wind blows the clouds overhead...
And catches the sail on the surfboard!
Just hold on—you have nothing to dread!!

The surfboard takes off like an arrow
Being shot from a fine archer's bow...
But there is no real prearranged target!
The surfer decides where to go.

What an expert at changing direction,
As if guided by Nature's commands...
So agile in riding his surfboard,
So majestic in flight, there he stands!

Hold on tight! For he's now going airborne
As he once again changes his course...
And heads for the beach just like light'ning,
While fighting centrifugal force!

What a ride! Did you get some great photos?
I sure hope you weren't TOO scared.
After all, you've had quite an adventure!
Thank the surfer who it with us shared!

A windsurfer checking his board at the beach

Windsurfer entering the water to begin his ride

A recent addition to surfing activities in the islands is the sport of kite surfing. While watching several kite surfers in action on the beach at the Maui Schooner Resort in Kihei, Maui, I tried to imagine the excitement associated with this sport—and my thoughts resulted in an effort to describe…

A Kite Surfer's Dream

My surfboard seemed lighter than ever
As it screamed across fields of white foam,
Challenging me not to lose balance
As over the waves I did roam.

The sun was near the horizon;
Daylight would soon come to an end:
The prevailing Tradewinds would then lessen,
Taking with them the surfer's best friend….

Then a gust of air found a pocket,
Surrounded by my crescent-shaped kite.
Lifting me up through the waves' crest:
What a feeling as I now was in flight!

The sun had now reached the horizon
And those fields of white foam turned to gold.
My kite, suspended in the sunset sky,
Was now quite a sight to behold.

Its surface reflected the sun's golden rays,
While lifting me high in the air.
Taking the image of a Fall's Harvest Moon,
Inviting others their sweet dreams to share.

Kite surfer on the beach of the Maui Sunset Resort in Kihei, Maui

As a writer, I spend a lot of time observing activities that occur in Nature. One experience in Hawaii showed me the excitement and the joy of young native birds who, following the advice of their parents, take part in a breakfast buffet being served on a beachside lawn: a meal worth waiting for as the birds...

Follow That Lawnmower

Today is the day, my children:
Be prepared for what's to come!
The lawnmower's engine has started:
Be alert and don't act dumb!

After hours of exercise and training
Of the legs, the eyes, and the beaks,
Show Mom how much you've accomplished
In the nest these past three weeks!
Fly down and get into position,
For the testing's about to begin.
The cutting of the lawn is the challenge:
Run swiftly! That's how you will win.

FOLLOW THAT LAWNMOWER! Quickly!
Don't delay, or you'll miss a fine meal
As the blades startle insects and earthworms
Who no longer themselves can conceal.

Run like the gecko! Be agile!
Use your beak! Like the shark, take the prize!!
Just remember, as you capture and swallow...
Your stomachs may be smaller than your eyes.

Birds following the lawnmower

Early morning at the SeaWatch Restaurant in Wailea, Maui

What an introduction to the daily life of tourists and of local island inhabitants. As I traveled around the islands, getting better acquainted with the people and with the culture of Hawaii, I began to appreciate…

A Pen's Delight

Observe the formation of a rainbow
While standing in the rain;
Follow the flight of the sugarcane ash
While sitting in a field of cane;
Chart the flight of the puffy white clouds
While watching them scamper below;
Imagine the source of the cresting waves
As the water moistens your toe;
Sketch the image of the swaying palms
As hammocks in the Tradewinds rock;
Wave to the passengers on board a ship
As it gracefully departs from the dock;
Let your imagination run wild
While relaxing on a scenic lanai…
Only then will you capture the feeling of a pen
As a writer describes life passing by.

Fisherman at Port Allen Beach, Kauai

As my final "stop" in my introduction to this collection of poems and photographs, I wish to provide some thoughts about the word "Aloha". I came across a little booklet entitled *The Aloha Spirit*, put together by Dr. Serge King, the Executive Director of Aloha International and internationally known speaker who lives on the Garden Island of Kauai. The booklet, released in 1990, begins with the following statements:

- "THE ALOHA SPIRIT is a well-known reference to the attitude of friendly acceptance for which the Hawaiian Islands are so famous. However, it also refers to a powerful way to resolve any problem, accomplish any goal, and also to achieve any state of mind or body that you desire."

- "In the Hawaiian language, ALOHA stands for much more than just 'hello' or 'goodbye' or 'love'. Its deeper meaning is 'the joyful (oha) sharing (alo) of the life energy (ha) in the present (alo)'."

- "As you share this energy, you become attuned to the Divine Power that the Hawaiians call MANA (a word that indicates that 'all Power comes from within'). And the loving use of this incredible Power is the secret for attaining true health, happiness, prosperity and success."

Now let's begin our travels around the islands, allowing me, the writer, to give you, the reader, a glimpse of "life passing by" as I provide you "a fleeting glimpse of Paradise".

Kite surfer at Sunset: Maui Schooner Resort

View of SS *Independence* from Aloha Tower in Honolulu, Oahu

Getting Acquainted with the Islands: Memories of a Seven-Day Cruise on the SS Independence

When I first came to the Hawaiian Islands in 1973, I traveled with a group of educators on a special NEA summer tour to the island of Oahu. In 1974, I took part in a second NEA tour, staying on the islands of Oahu and Maui. These two organized tours gave me the chance to become acquainted with the islands...but only from a "tourist's" perspective. I returned to Hawaii in the 1980s but traveled only to Maui. I fell in love with this island but had not as yet experienced life on the islands of Kauai and Hawaii. Therefore, I decided to take a cruise that would offer me exposure to Oahu, Kauai, Maui, and Hawaii.

For anyone who enjoys the adventure and the excitement of a cruise, the seven-day Hawaiian Island Cruise, aboard the SS *Independence*, is a fabulous way in which to be introduced to the islands. Not only does the passenger learn about the history and the culture of each island, but he or she also has the chance to get acquainted with some individuals from the islands who make Hawaiian history and culture come to life.

When I first came on board, I was greeted by the Cruise Director, Erik Kyu Kawika Kamana'opono Hattori, who spoke to the passengers about the many activities that would take place on board during the week. Kamana'o was raised on Oahu and is a world-renowned hula dancer, twice receiving the award as Best Male Hula Dancer of the year—in 1993 and again in 1995. He is also an accomplished owner / handler of Pomeranians.

I took my first cruise on board the SS *Independence* in 1996 and then came back again in 1998 and in 2000. During the October 1998 cruise, I composed a poem as a salute to...

Author Burgess takes the wheel during his 1998 cruise

Kamana'o Hattori: A Cruise Director and More

When you decide to take your vacation
Cruising the islands of Hawaii,
You are certain to strike up a friendship
With Kamana'o Hattori.
Kamana'o is the cruise ship director,
But he's really a lot more than that!
He conducts the Sunday church service
And often will sit down and chat,
Telling us how he learned hula…
Then became a World Champion—TWICE!

Kamana'o shows great pride in his culture
And these days, that is something quite nice.
His energy is very contagious:
He soon has us all on our feet,
Applauding the ship's entertainers—
HANA HO we will often repeat!

Kamana'o is a great cruise director,
For he does more than simply direct.
He participates in all the activities:
Not one does he ever neglect.
In this way, he spreads kindness and friendship
As only Kamana'o can…
Being part of the Spirit of Aloha:
"Kamana'o, you're the cruise 'Superman'!"

Cruise Director Kamana'o Hattori joins passengers in a hula rehearsal

During the cruise, passengers are entertained AND educated by a number of talented individuals—from educators (kumus) to singers to dancers. One individual who made a special impression with me was the ship's kumu, Haunani Kaui. Haunani was raised on Kauai and has been working as an entertainer since the age of sixteen for her family business, Smith's Boat Service, taking daily tours to the Fern Grotto. She toured the world, singing for Hawaiian Airlines. Haunani has performed with the Apana Sisters, with Aunty Genoa Keawe, and with Val Kepalino. She also is considered one of the top upright bass players of Hawaii.

On my 1998 cruise, I dedicated a special poem to…

Haunani Kaui: Kumu and Singer

The talents of kumu Haunani
Are well known to friends, far and near,
And those whom she's met on the cruise ship
Take home mem'ries that forever stay dear.
Her knowledge of culture and history
She shares in a quite unique way,
Reflecting the "Spirit of Aloha"
Of a people who live every day
Proud of their cultural heritage
And eager to share it with joy
With the visitors who come to the islands—
Most strangers to both hula and poi.

Haunani is a talented musician
Who performs on guitar in fine style…
And when she begins to "talk story",
On each face there appears a bright smile.

When YOU come to the islands of Hawaii—
To spend seven days on a cruise—
Say "Aloha" to gifted Haunani:
She will help chase away all your blues.

Haunani Kaui entertains passengers during a cruise on the SS *Independence*

SS *Independence* kumus Kahea and Haunani

Kamana'o and Haunani not only inspired me to compose poetry about them and about their contributions to the success of a seven-day cruise on board the SS *Independence*, but also gave me a good reason for signing up for two more cruises between 1998 and 2001.

Another member of the entertainment staff on the SS *Independence* is a performer whose talents as guitarist and singer are unique. Not only does he have a four-octave vocal range, but also is able to perform for more than nine hours WITHOUT repeating any musical number—and—he performs WITHOUT the use of sheet music as a guide. This entertainer's name is Butch Niahoe Kekaulike Kahakauila O'Sullivan, and there is one sentence in Hawaiian that Butch uses to synopsize his music: "Ho'okani au i ke mele no ka ho'omaika'i ana i ka honua." It means he plays music to make the world a better place.

Butch learned to play music because his folks had parties all the time and everyone sang, danced, and played music. His formal training is as an artist. He has a degree in Fine Arts and taught at the Institute of American Indian Arts in Santa Fe, New Mexico, for a year.

When I learned this entertainer and I have something in common—we both have a butterfly as a symbol—I had no difficulty in composing...

A Salute to Butch O'Sullivan

I was sailing on the SS *Independence*
On a seven-day, four-island trip.
As a member of the Holokai Hui Club,
I was one of the first on board ship,
Spending more than an hour in the Kama'aina Lounge
Enjoying a concert in song
Performed by a talented musician—
I could have listened to his voice all day long.

Butch O'Sullivan is the name of this singer
Who welcomed the passengers that day.

His talents as singer and guitarist
Made us all feel at home right away
As he took us on a musical journey
To the islands of Hawaii, and beyond,
While extending the "Spirit of Aloha"—
Of his music we became very fond.

All week long he appeared on the cruise ship—
From the Surfrider Bar and the pool
To the Captain's Gala Reception—
Entertaining like a sparkling jewel
With a range from bass to falsetto
And a repertoire rich and diverse:
Each performance created fond mem'ries
As his songs through the ship did traverse.

I discovered we had something in common,
This talented singer and I:
We both use an image from Nature—
The delicate, yet strong, butterfly—
As we talk about lifetime adventures
That have lifted our spirits on high,
Sharing in song and in poetry
The joys that make our spirits "fly".

Butch O'Sullivan is a special performer,
One who takes life right in stride
As he entertains both friends and tourists,
With a little "talk story" on the side.
"Mahalo, Butch, for the memories
That helped make my cruise week complete.
As a writer and teacher, I salute you!
I'm so pleased that on board we did meet."

Butch O'Sullivan, his record producer Bob Brown, and Author Burgess

Butch and two of his many fans

Butch O'Sullivan prepares to entertain guests during Hawaiian Island Cruise

As you can tell from the photo on the previous page, the smile of Butch O'Sullivan says volumes about his personality as an entertainer. After I composed the poem for Butch on the 1998 cruise, we kept in touch and I became a member of his fan club. I had the opportunity to participate in a cruise in the Caribbean in October of 2000—a cruise on which Butch was the featured entertainer. During that seven-day cruise, I was inspired to compose a poem about...

The Musical Journey of Butch O'Sullivan

With the butterfly as his symbol
Butch O'Sullivan flutters by,
Living life to its fullest—
Not conforming to any set die.
Singing, whistling, and yodeling,
While accompanying himself on guitar,
Butch shows us the beauty that we each have within
As we learn more about who we are.
He doesn't know where God will lead him
On the roads that he'll travel up ahead:
He enjoys all the adventures he encounters,
Taking time some "Aloha" to spread.
Butch's music entertains and enlightens
For, just like the butterfly in flight,
It brings to mind memories of caterpillar dreams
That now have become winged delights.

As I mentioned earlier, the butterfly image is something that Butch O'Sullivan and I have in common. Butch has a fan club newsletter called "Flutter By-Lines," in which he often gives examples of those "caterpillar dreams" that evolve into "winged delights."

Several years ago, I composed a poem about some butterflies that were flying around a butterfly bush in my backyard in Audubon, New Jersey. That poem is one of my most requested works, and I take the liberty of presenting it at this point. It is called...

A Butterfly with a Wrinkled Wing

My friends say that I'm handicapped because I'm not like they.
They flutter off when I come near...and with them I can't play.
But there is nothing wrong with me; there's just one minor thing:
I am a tiger swallowtail who has a wrinkled wing.

I fly as high and far as they, and pollinate as well...
But that one blemish on my wing does more than words can tell.
It labels me as something weird that doesn't fit the "mold"...
And thus I'm forced to fly alone, through skies both warm and cold.

I know they'll never understand what damage they have done
By choosing not to fly with me...for they just think it's fun!
If only I could make them see that beauty is "wing deep",
While talent and ability are traits we ALL can reap!

But I'll not let them get me down and make me feel ashamed.
I'll simply work much harder to prove that I'm not maimed!
For I'm as good and strong as they, unique in just one thing:
I am that tiger swallowtail who has a wrinkled wing.

Soon after I wrote this poem, I shared it with some of my students at Cherry Hill High School EAST in Cherry Hill, New Jersey, where I spent my entire twenty-six-year teaching career as a Spanish instructor. The students told me the poem was "autobiographical" in nature. When I asked them to explain, they pointed out that I was bald when I began teaching at EAST—at the age of twenty-two—and that, for two years, I wore a hairpiece. They saw baldness as my "wrinkle" and that "flying alone, through skies both warm and cold" led me to the decision to wear a toupee.

The butterfly thus became a symbol for me and one that I have seen reflected in the thoughts of Butch O'Sullivan, who encourages his readers of "Flutter By-Lines" to "do the best YOU can and success will follow."

I shall now present highlights of one of my seven-day Hawaiian cruises. One of the exciting moments of the cruise is the departure. On one of my cruises, I was on board during Hawaiian Heritage Week. As a result, members of a local island hula school were on board and the young passengers participated in the "streamer-throwing event" as the SS *Independence* departed from the island of Oahu. One of the young students was covered with streamers by his friends and I, camera in hand (as always), took his picture. This moment inspired me to compose a salute to Kawika Kaui and to name him the official "Cruise Mascot."

Kawika Kaui (Cruise Mascot)

Kawika Kaui: Rainbow Streamer
Cruise Mascot of the SS Independence

It is said that for every fine school or great team
A mascot is a must:
An entity
That's filled with glee
And a symbol folks can trust.
The SS *Independence* of the American Hawaii Line
Has searched both far and near—
On ev'ry isle
For quite a while—
To find a mascot to cheer.
The birth of the cruise ship's mascot so fine
Took place Hawaiian Heritage Week:
Saturday night,
Full moon in sight,
Letting everyone near Diamond Head peek.
As part of the departure ceremony,
In which most passengers took part,
Streamers were thrown;
Friendship was shown;
Another island adventure did start.
That October 3rd evening in 1998
Many streamers fell back to the deck,
Finding David…
And, as they did,
Cov'ring his whole body from his toes to his neck.
That's how the cruise ship's fine mascot was born,
The result of the joy that is shown:
Sailing the seas;
Feeling the breeze;
Seeing how the "Spirit of Aloha" has grown.

The name "Rainbow Streamer" seems perfect, indeed,
For this mascot that reflects what is done
On board the ship
On ev'ry trip,
Bringing friendship and joy in ways that are fun!

The staff of the ship gives thanks to the youth
Who created this great entity:
NA HULA-O
KAOHIKU—
KAPULANI... Hula dancers, you see.
They were part of the ship's entertainment
That October Hawaiian Heritage Week.
They made us smile
With their great style—
And for years we of them shall speak.

A special "Mahalo" is extended by all
To KAWIKA, the mascot supreme.
He gave his all!
Now he stands tall
As the symbol reflecting the great cruise ship's dream!

Since that special evening in 1998, I have kept in contact with Kawika Kaui
and his family. Kawika invited me to come to his school on the island of Kauai,
an experience that will be shared later in this collection of poems and photos.
On the following page, I share with you several photos of Kawika and his family that were taken between 1999 and 2003....

Kawika Kaui and his family

Trinette Kaui and son Donovan surprise Author Burgess at Borders Books
in Lihue, Kauai, attending the signing session for his book on patriotism

On another cruise, a talented group of students from Monta Vista High School in Cupertino, California, was part of the featured entertainment. The group— The Impressions—was accompanied by the director and the school's assistant principal. The performance on the final evening of the cruise inspired...

A Salute to "The Impressions"

On my cruise of the islands of Hawaii—
In April of the year ninety-eight—
My friends and my teaching colleagues
In the orchid room each evening ate.

A talented group of young students
Entertained us at dinner each night:
The Impressions from Monta Vista High School.
Their songs were, indeed, a delight.

Erin Paul is the choir's director.
(It's her first year at Monta Vista High.)
The trip was arranged by Assistant Principal Joanne Laird.
She's so proud of each gal and each guy!

The twenty-five voices in this choir—
Who call Cupertino, California, their home—
Gave performances on Kauai and on Maui
As part of their tour far from home.

On the final night of the cruise trip,
A great Gershwin medley was sung
In the cruise ship's Hoi Hoi Showplace
By this group of fine talents so young.

The passengers stood up and applauded!
(Many even kept shouting: "ENCORE!")
'Twas a night they will always remember,
Long after they've returned to shore.

Another traditional activity on board takes place on the final night of each cruise, just before sunset. The SS *Independence* sets sail from Kona, Hawaii, on Friday evening for the return to Oahu. A lei-tossing ceremony is held. If the flower leis float back toward the beach, it indicates that the person who threw the lei into the waters will return to Hawaii someday. The ceremony itself gives all the passengers the experience of...

Sunset and Aloha in Kona, Hawaii

The passengers on the SS *Independence*
Had recently returned to the ship,
Being tendered from Kona, Hawaii,
On the last day of a four-island trip.
Kamana'o and Haunani, the kumu,
Had gathered on Ohana Deck, Aft,
To prepare for the lei-tossing ceremony
As the crew was securing the raft
That was used as the "floating connector"
From the ship to the tender that day.
There were tears in the eyes of the passengers
As they created an immense flower lei
That was thrown from the deck into the waters
That caress the Kona shoreline...
And as the cruise ship departed,
Sailing into a sunset divine,
The skies became filled with bright colors—
Yellows and purples and reds.
'Twas a picturesque scene of Aloha,
A sunset that memories spread
O'er the eight hundred on board the cruise ship
Who soon would return to their homes—
Memories of glorious adventures
On the islands where the gecko still roams.
As the sun softly touched the horizon,
Then quickly departed from sight,
The passengers joined hands in friendship...
As the ship sailed off into the night.

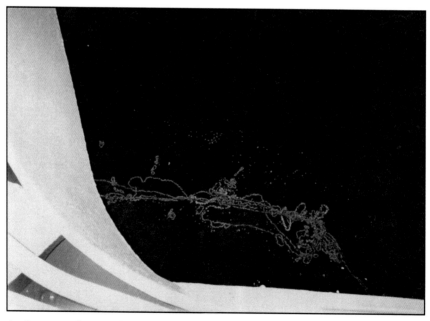

And now, a photo collage of events and activities aboard the SS *Independence*

SS *Independence* cruises past the USS *Arizona* Memorial. The *Arizona* was sunk by the Japanese on Sunday, December 7, 1941. The crewmembers are still interred there where they lost their lives.

Na Hula O Kaohikukapulani, members of a Hula Halau from Kauai, performed on the SS *Independence* in 1998

Author Burgess shares his poetry with passengers on board the SS *Independence* in April 1998

I visited the island of Maui in February of 2001 and took time to go to the harbor in Kahului to once again see the SS *Independence*—in her new home-port. She looked as majestic as ever, docked along the pier. The image brought back memories of my four cruises, and I looked forward to the day when I would again come on board.

Little did anyone know what would happen in late 2001. I was on Maui on September 11 of that year. When I returned again, in February of 2002, I learned that, because of the events that took place on September 11, 2001, the American Hawaii Cruise Lines had gone out of business—and the SS *Patriot* and the SS *Independence* would no longer cruise the islands. Within a year, the growth that was shown was completely taken away, and as I walked along the pier at the Kahului Harbor, it seemed so strange to realize that...

And Then ... There Were None

I set sail on the SS *Independence*
Four times in the past ten years.
The memories will last me a lifetime:
The friendships, the music, scenic piers.
Yet today, when I visited the ship's Port of Call
In Kahului, Maui, I shed tears....
The beautiful ship and her wonderful staff
May never bring more joy to my ears.

The cruise line had been so successful
From 1997 to 1999
That a decision was made to add a new ship:
The SS *Patriot* was made part of the line.
She made her first cruise in December,
The year 2000 thus ended in style.
She didn't have the "character" of the SS *Constitution*,
But to her guests she brought many a smile.

No one could foresee what would happen
In October of 2001:
The terrorist attacks on September 11
Took away dreams of Hawaii cruise fun....
And so, by the end of two thousand one,
A state of bankruptcy was declared.
No longer would the two ships sail proudly
Through the waters, as Aloha was shared.

As I walked along the cruise ship's dock,
Dressed in my red, white, and blue,
On that February afternoon
In the calendar year two thousand two,
I recalled those cherished memories
Of the voyages on that proud little ship....

Kamana'o Hattori, Hula Champion
And Cruise Director on each trip;

Haunani Kaui, the kumu
Each day she'd "talk story" and sing;
Entertainer extraordinaire Butch O'Sullivan,
Oh, the joy his melodies would bring!

Those memories brought a bright smile to my face
As I left the dock that day.
For the special gift of ALOHA I'd received
Can never be taken away.

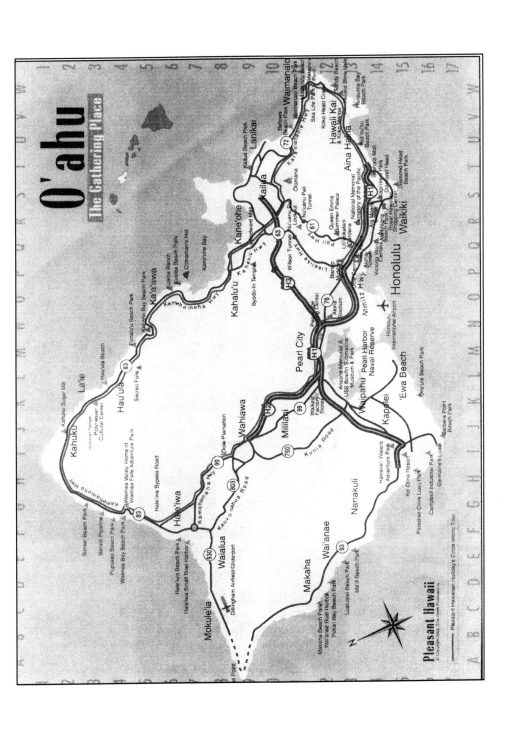

O'ahu
The Gathering Place

Pleasant Hawaii
© Copyright 2004, The Week Publications

—— Pleasant Hawaiian Holidays Circle Island Tour

Now that you have a "taste" of the excitement and of the beauty of Hawaii, I shall take you on an island-by-island visual and literary tour. I shall begin on the island of Oahu, known as the "Gathering Place". From there, we shall travel to Kauai, "The Garden Isle"; to Hawaii, "The Big Island"; and to Maui, "The Valley Isle". The final part of the journey will show the patriotic spirit of the people. The tour begins as I, the writer and photographer, call you, the reader, to come on board in the typical Hawaiian way; blowing the conch shell...

Aerial view of Diamond Head Crater

Aerial view of Honolulu and of Waikiki Beach (right) on the island of Oahu

O'ahu: The Gathering Place

Before the 1990s, when airport expansion projects on Hawaii and on Maui made direct flights from the Mainland possible, Oahu was the first stop for all visitors to the islands. This is how the island got the nickname "The Gathering Place". When most people hear the word "Oahu" mentioned in a conversation, the first images that come to mind are Pearl Harbor and the *Arizona* Memorial; Waikiki Beach; the famous view of Diamond Head Crater that overlooks Waikiki Beach; and the beaches along the north shore of the island, so well known as the best surfing sites in the world. The two most recognizable figures associated with Oahu are entertainer Don Ho and the star of the 1960s -1970s TV show *Hawaii Five-0*, Jack Lord (Police Chief Steve McGarrett).

On my literary tour, I shall begin at the site of the *Arizona* Memorial at Pearl Harbor. I first visited the site in December of 1996—fifty-five years after the attack on Pearl Harbor by the Japanese on December 7, 1941. The experience is one I shall never forget. The most memorable vision was that of oil from the USS *Arizona* that still continues to escape from the ship and rise to the surface. I returned for a second visit on September 5, 2001. I had come to Pearl Harbor to greet the members of the crew of the USS *Benfold* as the ship returned from a six-month deployment in Pacific waters. I brought along a poet and publisher from Wenatchee, Washington, Mrs. Ella M. Dillon, the owner of Redrosebush Press. She had not seen the memorial, so we visited the site just before greeting the USS *Benfold*, a ship named for a Medal of Honor recipient from Audubon, New Jersey, Navy Corpsman Edward C. Benfold, killed in action in Korea on September 5, 1952.

My visit to the *Arizona* Memorial on December 21, 1996, inspired me to compose a poetic tribute to…

The Men of the USS Arizona: America's Special Heroes

Every race and culture has at least one special place
Where its heroes have been honored with a patriotic embrace.
It may be in a special park in the nation's capitol,
Created to remind us of those who gave their all
Fighting for the freedom of the citizens of the race,
Struggling when the odds were great in a strange, foreboding place.

The citizens of the U.S.A. have honored those who died
With very special monuments that reflect the nation's pride:
The tomb of soldiers, names unknown, who lost their lives in war;
A wall containing names of those killed in the Vietnam War;
A battlefield with statues representing all the troops—
From Army, Navy, Air Force, Marines, and Coast Guard Groups—
Who fought and died heroically, fighting for world peace,
In the nation of Korea, in the hope that war would cease.

Yet there is one memorial that stands out from the rest:
It's located in Pearl Harbor—on the waters it does rest—
Above the USS *Arizona*, a Naval battleship
Destroyed and sunk while anchored, NOT by an enemy ship.
Unlike other monuments that help our memories last,
The *Arizona* Memorial contains memories from the past...
From Sunday, December 7, in 1941
When the Japanese invaded with the dawning of the sun.

It is a LIVING memorial, constructed on the site
Where the crew of the *Arizona* was killed in the dawn's early light.
The names on the wall of this memorial are those whose bodies lay
In the ruins of the battleship—near the entrance to the bay—
That rests beneath the memorial, in waters that contain
America's special heroes, who in our hearts still remain.

Publisher Ella Dillon of Redrosebush Press visits Pearl Harbor: September 5, 2001

Author Burgess prepares to board the USS *Arizona* Memorial on September 5, 2001

I currently serve as the liaison from Audubon, New Jersey, to the U.S. Navy. I was both amazed and honored back in 1998 when I received an official invitation to come to San Diego, California, on Memorial Day (May 30) and to attend a special naval ceremony. It was an experience I shall always remember: attendance at…

The Commissioning of the USS Pearl Harbor

On Saturday morning, May 30—
The official Memorial Day—
More than five thousand people had gathered
For a ceremony on San Diego Bay.
The ceremony marked the commissioning
Of a new ship in the Navy's fine fleet:
The Commissioning of the USS *Pearl Harbor.*
(In the audience, there wasn't one empty seat.)

The day was quite special for those veterans
Who had served during World War II
And for those who had been at Pearl Harbor,
The event seemed too good to be true.
More than one thousand one hundred survivors
Of the attack that was heard "'round the world"
Gathered on Coronado Island
To relive what on December 7 had unfurled.

Dressed in colorful Aloha shirts
And white trousers, along with a lei,
They had come to celebrate the commissioning
Of the ship named in honor of that day…
Fifty-seven years after the bombing
That took place in 1941.
(Many a tear was shed by those
Who survived and were honored for deeds done.)

The commissioning took place in bright sunlight
And was followed by a reception on board:

The pride of the Navy was reflected that day
In the eyes of the crewmen who roared
As they followed the orders of the sponsor
Who gave the command, loud and clear,
To man their stations on board the ship—
It was the moment that finally was here!

None of those crewmen had yet been born
On Sunday, December 7, '41:
The knowledge they had of that moment in time
Came from readings in classrooms they'd done.
But for all of these modern-day sailors,
The role was one that was clear:
To honor the Pearl Harbor survivors
By their deeds—beginning this year.
Their actions, in peace and in wartime,
Will be a tribute to the spirit of all those
Who died while serving their country:
With each deployment their legacy grows.

I was there on that special Memorial Day.
I met survivors and saw
The incredible pride being showcased:
I listened to their stories in awe.

I, too, had not yet been born
When Pearl Harbor was attacked from the air,
But the memories of those gallant survivors
In my mind will always be there.
I was honored to attend the commissioning
Of the Navy's LSD 52
And am hoping this poetic tribute
Will help pass my pride on to YOU.

The crew of the USS *Pearl Harbor*
Is ready to serve our great land.
We, the citizens for whom they fight,
Must remember always to stand
And cheer for America's colors—

Our nation's bright RED, WHITE, AND BLUE.
Be patriotic and wave the flag proudly!
Always to your country be true!

Pearl Harbor survivor Gordon Jones, President of San Diego, California, Survivors' Chapter

Sailors line the decks of the USS *Pearl Harbor* during the commissioning ceremony on May 30, 1998, in San Diego

Many citizens from around the world who have never had the chance to come to Oahu in person were given the opportunity to see the island thanks to the long-running TV series, *Hawaii Five-0*. From 1968 until 1980, Steve McGarrett, the head of the fictitious police force known as Five-0, took viewers on excursions to many popular tourist sites while investigating crime on the island. The show is the longest-running crime series in TV history (thirteen years) and was seen in eighty countries, with an audience estimated at more than three hundred million. The series still appears in syndication.

Most viewers of the show remember the famous line McGarrett uttered as he looked at Dan Williams, his longtime second-in-command (played by James MacArthur), and said, "Book 'em, Danno!"

McGarrett (Jack Lord) passed away on Wednesday, January 21, 1998. For months I tried to find a way to express my thoughts about Lord and about the series. Finally, on Christmas Eve, 1998—while staying at the Papakea Resort, just north of the Kaanapali area on the island of Maui—I was able to write about...

The Death of Danno's Boss

As I sat on my living room carpet,
Cutting coupons for Valentine's Day,
I heard on an Action News Telecast
That an actor had just passed away.
It wasn't just ANY TV actor
Whose name was mentioned that day:
It was the Chief of Police in Hawaii,
Steve McGarrett, who each week came our way
In the longest-running crime series
Ever telecast on national TV,
Seen for thirteen years—in eighty countries—
'Twas the crime show all wanted to see!
The name of this crime show was *Hawaii Five-0*
And the actor was, of course, Jack Lord...
Whose searing gaze and chiseled chin
By millions of fans were adored.
Steve McGarrett fought crime in Hawaii
In a show that was often fast-paced:
He was thorough, demanding, and well-spoken
While solving each case that he faced.

His partner, actor James MacArthur,
Played McGarrett's loyal "sidekick", it's true,
And viewers could always be certain
That an episode in the series was through
When McGarrett would arrive at a showdown,
With partner Dan Williams at his side,
And utter the words: "Book 'em, DANNO!":
Five-0 fans loved that phrase far and wide.
For it captured the essence of the series—
Those words with which most shows would end—
Reflecting the style of McGarrett,
And the trust in his partner and friend.

Jack Lord was a symbol of justice.
A detective, a cop through and through,
Representing so well law and order,
As well as the red, white, and blue.

Jack Lord (John Joseph Patrick Ryan)
Will long be remembered with pride
As the police chief who wouldn't be outsmarted:
From McGarrett NO criminal could hide!

I am placing, on the next page, the article that appeared in the *Courier-Post*, a daily paper in Southern New Jersey, on Friday, January 23, 1998, following the death of Jack Lord. I was fascinated to learn that Lord majored in Art at New York University and that he appeared on Broadway before taking on the role of Steve McGarrett.

'Five-O' star
Jack Lord dies

Associated Press

HONOLULU - TV star Jack Lord, the straight-arrow *Hawaii Five-O* crimebuster with the searing gaze, the chiseled chin and the laminated pompadour that never seemed to wilt in the tropical heat, has died at 77.

Lord, who died of congestive heart failure Wednesday at his home, starred in the TV series as Steve McGarrett, the  gruff head of a fictitious Hawaii police force known as Five-O. He also produced and sometimes directed the show, which ran on CBS from 1968 to 1980.

The show often ended with Lord telling his sidekick, played by James MacArthur, "Book 'em, Danno!"

Hawaii Five-O - the longest running crime series in TV history - was seen in 80 countries with an audience estimated at more than 300 million. Reruns continue on cable, giving rise to a new generation of fans.

Born John Joseph Patrick Ryan in New York City, Lord studied at the Neighborhood Playhouse in New York and the Actors Studio. He majored in Art at New York University. He appeared on Broadway before he went to Hollywood and appeared in a number of movies.

At the beginning of every episode of *Hawaii Five-0*, one of the images presented was that of Diamond Head, located near Waikiki Beach and a familiar landmark on the island of Oahu. At this point on our tour, I want to share several visual images of Diamond Head and of the famous tourist destination on Oahu, Waikiki Beach.

The Beach in Waikiki, near the Royal Hawaiian Hotel

Waikiki Beach and Diamond Head from the beach in front of the Waikiki
Outrigger Hotel

For visitors to Oahu, nothing can compare to the beauty of…

Sunset on Waikiki Beach

I was enjoying the Waikiki sunset
From the Outrigger Beach Hotel,
While dining at Chuck's Steak House,
A restaurant many locals know well.
The sun didn't need a rehearsal:
Her performance came quite naturally.
The sights and sounds in the background
Created a fond memory.
The changing colors on Diamond Head
Brought to mind Haleakala scenes;
The reflection of the sun in the water,
A masterpiece of blues and greens.
Tourists and locals had gathered
To observe the sunset from the beach:
Some swimming, some surfing, some sketching
Images of a world out of reach.
A conch shell announced the sun's setting
While torches were lighted by the pool;
An outrigger canoe returned to shore;
The breezes of the Tradewinds turned cool.
A group of local musicians
Was performing in slack-key style
In the hotel's Sunset Terrace:
They performed with a contagious bright smile.
As the sun sank below the horizon,
Passing cirrus clouds turned a golden hue—
While I started writing this poem
That I am now sharing with you.

View of sunset from the Outrigger Hotel on Waikiki Beach

Many veterans of World War II remember seeing Waikiki Beach when only one hotel was reflected in the waters along the beach: The Royal Hawaiian. Today this majestic structure, although hidden from view beyond the modern malls and shops located along Kalakaua Boulevard, still is recognized as...

The Pink Palace

I traveled to Waikiki this week
To see a dear friend of mine:
The beautiful Royal Hawaiian Hotel.
Had she stood the test of time?
With the nickname "The Pink Palace",
She reflected the sun's bright rays,
Glimmering on the pure white beach
From Septembers to Marches to Mays.

In the background, the mighty Diamond Head
Ruled the Waikiki skies.
I wondered whether the image had changed:
Was I in for a big surprise?
The last time I had seen her
Was in nineteen-forty-five:
World War II had just ended
And Oahu had come alive
To celebrate the victory
That would put an end to war.
The Royal Hawaiian was radiant...
Even more than she'd been before!

As I walked along Kalakaua Boulevard,
In search of my dear old friend,
I couldn't find a trace of her.
Had she met an untimely end?
And where, oh, where, was Diamond Head,
That landmark so well known?

I stopped at the International Market Place
And sat there all alone.

Hotels and shops were everywhere,
Yet one I could not see:
My beloved Royal Hawaiian
On the beach at Waikiki.

A local resident, walking by,
Perceived that I felt blue.
She stopped and asked from where I'd come…
And if there was something she could do.
I told her I could not find
A dear old friend of mine:
A friend I'd met in World War II—
"The Pink Palace", now lost in time.

"Dear Sir, she has not disappeared.
Let me show you where she lies,
On the pure white sands of Waikiki
In the sunlit, cloudless skies."

Hidden by a modern mall,
Her brilliance hasn't dimmed:
The Royal Hawaiian still reflects
An elegance that remains untrimmed.
And from her beach, proud Diamond Head
Still on the horizon stands,
Its majesty unchanged with time
Overlooking those pure white sands.

The Royal Hawaiian Hotel on Waikiki Beach
known affectionately by many as "The Pink Palace"

In August of 2003, I traveled beyond the limits of Honolulu for the first time...
to experience the "other" Oahu:

Oahu's North Shore: A Forty-five-Minute Drive— And a World Away—from Waikiki Beach

Oahu is known as "The Gathering Place"
And Honolulu reflects the name well:
Waikiki Beach and Diamond Head;
On each block at least one high-rise hotel.
Dozens of restaurants and souvenir shops
Can be seen on each side of the street;
Nearby is Pearl Harbor, an historic site,
With the USS *Arizona* beneath your feet.

Many visitors to Oahu remain in Waikiki,
Unaware of the treasures to be found
Less than an hour north and east of the city,
Where the variety of sites will astound:
The wonders of the Dole Pineapple Plantation;
The sacred grounds of an ancient Heiau;
The world-famous north shore surfing beaches;
A Turtle Beach Resort Luau.

For those wishing to learn about the cultures
That have been part of Hawaii's rich past,
A visit to the Polynesian Cultural Center
Will bring memories that forever will last.

As I complete my fleeting glimpse of this island Paradise, I present some visual
reflections of the ideas expressed in the poem you have just read...

One of the beaches at the Turtle Bay Resort

Waitress Virginia at the Turtle's Den Café at the Turtle Bay Resort shares a moment of Aloha with Author Burgess

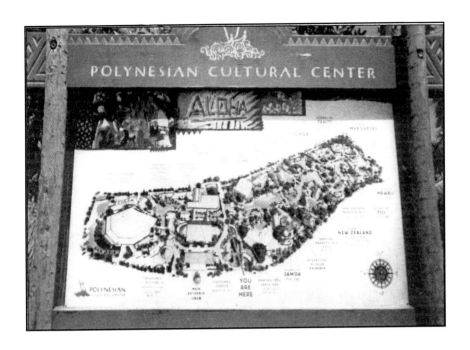

Visitors take a canoe ride through the Polynesian Cultural Center on Oahu

Easter Island display at the Polynesian Cultural Center

Performers prepare for presentation of Dance and Chant

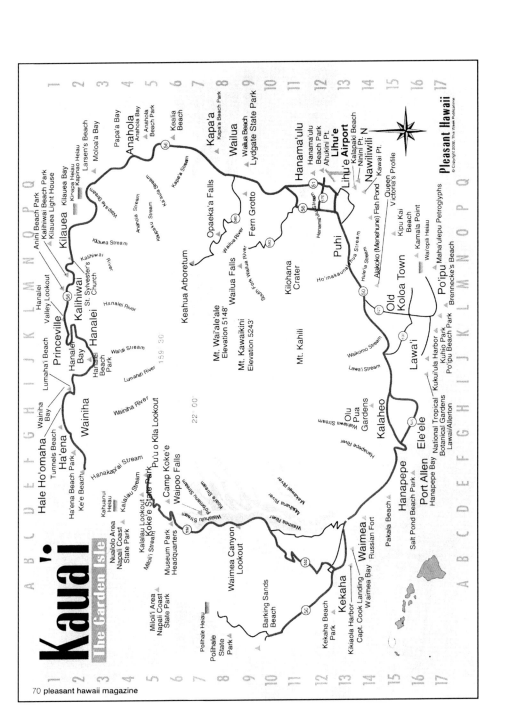

Kaua'i
The Garden Isle

Pleasant Hawaii
© Copyright 2006, The Week Publications

Welcome sign at Lihue Airport on Kauai

A familiar sight at Opaekaa Falls near Kapa'a, Kauai

Kauai

The best way to begin my tour of Kauai is with the poem I composed in December of 1995, following…

My First Visit to Kauai

My thirty-one hour adventure
On the fiftieth state's Garden Isle
Is one I shall always remember:
Just recalling it brings back a smile.

Many friends were made on that visit—
At Borders and at Waimea High—
And when I return to New Jersey,
Flying five thousand miles through the sky,
I'll have much to discuss with my colleagues—
At East and at Audubon High:
There'll be photos and other great mem'ries…
Including my Santa Claus tie!

'Twas the fourteenth day of December
In the calendar year '95,
When I first set foot on the island
That is known by the name of Kauai.

I spent my first day on the island
Seeing some places well known.
I went to the scenic Fern Grotto,
Where Nature her beauty is shown
In the heart of the Wailua River,
Whose banks are caressed by the breeze,
Blowing through Hau limbs and palm fronds,
Setting one's spirit at ease.
I also drove up the main highway
To Princeville, and even beyond,
Where I had to cross eight one-lane bridges!
(Of those I became very fond!)

I had come to attend a book signing,
And a poetry reading as well,
For *Once upon a Lifetime,*
A book in which much I did tell:
The life of a high school instructor,
both inside and outside his class;
Adventures in faraway places;
Predictions... would they all come to pass?

The signing took place at a Borders
Which had opened just three months before.
Mary Daubert, community liaison,
Had invited me to come to her store
To share with her poetry readers
My visions and thoughts on the world—
As well as discuss other projects
Which, over the years, had unfurled
While I worked as a Spanish instructor
In a high school named Cherry Hill EAST.
What a fabulous evening of sharing!
And it lasted three hours, at least!

Mary Daubert showed why she's successful
In the work that she does on Kauai:
She made some special arrangements,
With a teacher at Waimea High,

For me to spend time in some classes.
How could I say no to this chance
To speak to the youth of the island,
As well as my knowledge enhance
Of the daily routine of a teacher
Who works on a tropical isle?

I spent the whole day at the high school
And even spoke Spanish for a while!
My host for this seven-hour visit
Teaches English at Waimea High.
He allowed me to speak with his classes:
Wow! How the hours flew by!

Shannon Hart is the name of this teacher
Who served as my host for this day.
He was born on the island of Oahu,
Just twenty-nine air minutes away
From his home on the isle of Kauai,
Where he teaches—and coaches as well.
Mr. Hart takes great pride in his teaching:
His students know that—you can tell!

The day that I spoke with his classes,
The door to his classroom looked great:
Covered with bright decorations…
His students had helped decorate.
That door has been entered in a contest.
Will it soon be picked as the best?
(As I walked here and there on the campus,
To me it outclasses all the rest!)

I served as a Mainland ambassador
On my trip to Waimea High,
Bringing copies of student newspapers.
(I am sure you can understand why.)
Students in the state of New Jersey
Were hoping to make some new friends,
Sharing ideas and stories—

As well as some fads and some trends—
Unique to the state and the cities
In which they were born and then raised.
Of course they could learn from each other…
And, at times, be simply amazed
At the daily routines being followed
By students in each of the schools:
Yes! The climate does indeed make a difference
In the setting of guidelines and rules!

Mr. Hart gave me a great present
To give to my students back home:
A copy of the recent *Perspectives*,
A very informative tome.
It contained both short stories and poems,
Filled with some mem'rable "views",
Covering a number of topics…
Composed both to teach and amuse.

I learned in detail about Iniki,
Whose winds o'er the isle cruelly blew
On that infamous September 11
In the calendar year '92,
Destroying the homes and the buildings,
Reshaping Kauai in its wake.
The students wrote vivid descriptions:
What a mess that hurricane did make!

Many poems included a stanza
That referred to a bright ray of hope
That filled all the island's inhabitants,
As each through the rubble did grope.
Their hope was expressed in a saying
That is well understood on Kauai:
That marvelous "Spirit of Aloha"
Was to help everyone to survive!

It helped provide strength to the victims,
As they struggled to rebuild their lives,

And gave them a positive outlook:
That's how everyone works and survives.

The other short stories and poems
Were descriptions of everyday life:
Of the fears and the joys of the people;
Of their feelings on peace and on strife.

"Mahalo, Mr. Hart, for that present...
And my students will be thanking you, too,
For they'll learn how the youth of Kauai
Survived in the year '92—
And how the young men and young women
On the beautiful isle of Kauai
Have confronted those everyday problems
That have caused them to laugh and to cry."

When I fin'ly returned to the airport,
After spending the day at the school,
I posed by the plane for a photo,
Then returned to the Schooner's warm pool
On the Valley Isle known as Maui,
Where I wrote of my trip to Kauai
While watching a colorful sunset
In the tropical skies of Hawaii.

English teacher Shannon Hart
of Waimea High School
welcomes Author Burgess to his
classroom in December 1995

Spanish Class at Waimea High School displays piñatas during December 1995 visit by Author (and former Spanish instructor from New Jersey) Burgess

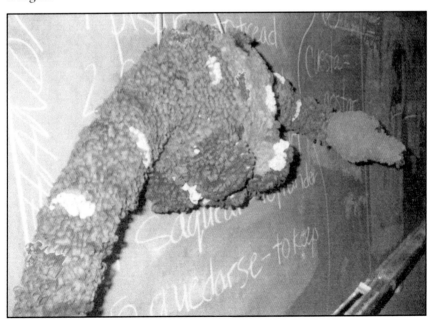

I met Mary Daubert over the Labor Day weekend in 1995 while attending my first Maui Writers' Conference. We both attended one of the sessions on poetry at the conference and, when she heard that I had just had a book signing for a book of poetry at a Borders Books & Music location in New Jersey, asked whether I would be interested in coming to her new store in Lihue, Kauai, which was scheduled to open in late October of 1995. Mrs. Daubert didn't tell me that she had contacted Waimea High School. When I came to the book signing, she introduced me to Mr. Hart and then told me that arrangements had been made for me to spend the next day at the school, sharing some of my work with the students in English classes. (In my book *Once upon a Lifetime: A Teacher's Eye View of Living in the World Today*, an entire section focuses on Hawaii, with ten poems and four photographs. This is why Mrs. Daubert asked me to come to Kauai for the signing and sharing session.) Because of her kindness, I could not prepare a book about the islands without including...

A Salute to Mary Daubert

When a company hires employees,
It will always endeavor to find
Individuals who have personality,
Who are patient, understanding, and kind.
The manager of Borders Books & Music
In Lihue, on the island of Kauai,
Reflects well these traits sought in hiring:
Mary Daubert is the best! And here's why:
She's creative in setting up signings
For authors who appear at her store,
Using techniques that flatter their talents—
Special flyers, display tables, and more.
Mary also makes certain she's present
When an author or musician arrives,
Greeting the guest with "Aloha";
To make them feel at home, she strives!
Mary Daubert, as a poet I salute you
And I know that Borders must be proud
To have you as one of its managers:
You help Borders stand out in the crowd!

Poetry sharing session at Borders Books in Lihue, Kauai: December
1995

Mary Daubert, Community Relations Coordinator at Borders Books in
Lihue, greets Author Burgess in December 1995

Another Flower Lei Greeting awaits on the February 2001 visit

This poem was composed for Mary after my second book signing at her Lihue, Kauai, location. The signing sessions gave me a wonderful opportunity to spend more time on Kauai and to get to know more about "The Garden Isle". I attended signing sessions in 1995, in 1997, and again in 2001. On this 2001 visit, I learned that Mary would be leaving Borders, having accepted a position as the Public Relations Chairperson for the largest shopping center on the island.

On another visit to Kauai, I traveled south and west in order to explore the wonders of Waimea Canyon, often referred to as "The Grand Canyon of the Pacific". On my way to Waimea Canyon, I passed through Hanapepe, "Kauai's Biggest Little Town", and stopped in for lunch at…

The Green Garden

When a visitor comes to the Garden Isle
For a week, or for just a few days,
He or she should visit Hanapepe
On Route 50, for it deserves lots of praise.
Hanapepe is Kauai's "Biggest Little Town"
And the "Bougainvillea Capital of Hawaii".
Many treasures can be found in Hanapepe…
Like the quaint restaurant famous on Kauai.
It's a restaurant that's been there for decades
And a place that's well known far and wide.
The name of the place: The Green Garden.
Locals mention the name with great pride!

When you enter this open-air restaurant,
You are surrounded—wherever you sit—
By flowers and plants and fine artwork:
No wonder it's the locals' favorite.
The meals that are served are so "ono"
And the service is second to none;
While dining, local music is playing;
The homemade pies can NOT be outdone!

You'll be treated as part of the "ohana"
When you go to The Green Garden to dine,
So stop by and say "Aloha" to Sue or to Gwen:
Then experience a meal that's divine!!

I then arrived at Waimea Canyon and spent several hours walking around and observing the wonders of the region. Anyone who visits this region will leave knowing that he or she has experienced…

The Essence of Kauai

They say when you come to Kauai,
There is one place you surely must see.
It is wide, it is deep, it is wondrous:
It's a place that's as green as can be.
This beautiful spot on the island
Can be reached from the airport in an hour…
And once you have reached the first lookout,
It will impress you with scenes of great power.

You can visit the Kokee Museum,
Or hike on a number of trails
That wander through natural beauty…
Bringing to mind ancient tales
Of the history and the culture of the island—
And of the people who have made it so great!
The place is called Waimea Canyon
And it's there lasting memories await.

Let me show some of the incredible beauty of Waimea Canyon…

Views of Waimea Canyon

By now, I am sure that you have noticed that, from time to time, I have placed a strange-looking word in the lines of one of my poems. These words are from the Hawaiian language, and I have used them because they express the meanings of the images much more clearly than the English translation. I wish to take a moment at this point in our travels to define several of these words. (Nothing like a Spanish teacher still thinking he is in the classroom....)

ALOHA	A full explanation for this word is seen in the introduction. However, the basic meanings are: "Hello", "Goodbye", "Love", and "Friendship".
OHANA	This is the Hawaiian word for "Family".
ONO	No meal in Hawaii can be enjoyed without saying "Delicious" at least five or six times.
MAHALO	This is the Hawaiian word for "Thank You."
MAHALO NUI LOA	"Thank You Very Much!"
NO KA OI	An expression that means "It's the Very Best."

Some spots on the island of Kauai receive more than six hundred inches of rain annually. This is one of the reasons for the name of "The Garden Isle" being used to refer to Kauai. On the next several pages, I shall take you on a journey around the island, with stops at the Fern Grotto, the Wailua River, and much, much more....

Leaving Waimea Canyon and driving east toward Waimea and Hanapepe, an almost hidden treasure awaits on the Oceanside of Waimea High School: a black sand beach located at Waimea Landing. During my September 2003 visit to Kauai, the Kaui family invited me to go fishing with some locals on the Waimea Landing Pier. The aweoweo were running—a small fish with a strong fish smell, used by the locals to prepare a crunchy, fried pupu. What an experience for me, a landlubber who does not enjoy fishing! A late Sunday afternoon of photography and of conversations with the local residents brought some unexpected memories. The locals explained that the run of aweoweo is seen as a sign of an advancing natural disaster. One such run of the fish occurred back in 1992—in September—just prior to the devastation caused by Hurricane Iniki. (On September 7,

2003, meteorologists were predicting possible landfall of Hurricane Jimena, but fortunately, the winds changed direction in time to avoid disaster.) I also learned about other fish in the area: the halalu, a sweeter fish than the aweoweo, and the opelu. The photographs on the next three pages clearly reflect the wonderful memories I have of that September afternoon....

The aweoweo, caught on the Waimea Recreational Pier, Sunday, September 7, 2003

Author Burgess brings in three aweoweo—with some great help from
some new friends—on the Waimea Pier

Continuing east toward Lihue, one comes to the town of Hanapepe, site of…

The Swinging Bridge of Hanapepe

With all of the things to see and to do
On the Garden Isle of Kauai,
Why would a wooden swinging bridge
Be on the list of must sites to see?

The bridge is located in Hanapepe,
The biggest little town on the isle,
And a walk across the wooden bridge
Is certain to produce a smile.

The walkway is made of wooden boards,
Each one about six inches wide,
In strips some three to four feet long,
All together with heavy wire tied.
There are no pillars or concrete supports,
So the bridge will sway to and fro
As the traveler begins the journey
O'er the rushing waters below.

My interest in this site is personal,
Since I live in a New Jersey town
Where a quaint swinging bridge stood for years
Before it was finally torn down.
Residents in Audubon who remember
Adventures on this bridge as a child
Aroused my curiosity…
Would MY adventure be so wild?

I enjoyed my walk on the swinging bridge
And I really wasn't too scared,
So when YOU travel to Hanapepe,
Take a walk on this bridge… if you dare!

Now, let's take a closeup view of this quaint site….

The swinging bridge in Hanapepe

In April of 2003, I was honored by the Kaui family on the island on Kauai when I received an invitation to attend a high school graduation (at the Kamehameha School on Oahu) and the graduation party for son Donovan (Kale) on Kauai. I attended the graduation party on May 31—an experience that inspired…

A Celebration for Kale Kaui

Many friends and relatives had gathered
On the Garden Isle of Kauai
To help celebrate—
In a way that was great—
A student's graduation from Kamehameha High.

The young man who was honored that evening
Greeted everyone with a smile,
Presenting a lei
As to each he would say
"Aloha" and "Mahalo" for stopping by for a while.

Entertainment for the party was provided
By hula dancers and by a musical band:
A wonderful night
Filled with delights
For Donovan Kaui, at a party well planned.

The event was a magical moment
For this New Jersey family friend.
I shall never forget
The new acquaintances I met…
And the memories of that party never will end.

Donovan and family

Donovan and dad

Donovan Kale Kaui has a love for his native language and culture. He was honored while a Senior at Kamehameha High School for a song he composed—in Hawaiian—for a young girl who lost her life at the age of fifteen, the victim of a tragic car accident on May 28, 2002.

Donovan has given me permission to include the words for his song, as well as some of his thoughts about the composition and its inspiration, in this collection of poems and photos. The words indeed reflect the culture as they tell a story. "Mahalo nui loa" to Donovan for allowing me to include this material in *A Fleeting Glimpse of Paradise.*

Ka Haku Mele
The Composer

Aloha kāua. My name is Kale Kau'i, and I am the composer of "Lilinoe." I am currently a senior at the Kamehameha Schools on O'ahu, although I come from Wailua Homesteads, Kaua'i. Throughout the school year, I board in 'Iolani Dormitory and come home on weekends and holidays to visit my 'ohana and friends. I have a deep love for the Hawaiian culture and have been studying the Hawaiian language for six years now. If it wasn't for the dedicated kumu ' lelo Hawai'i' (Hawaiian language teachers) at Kamehameha, I would have never been able to write this song. A big mahalo to them for opening the doors of opportunity for me and other haumāna (students) through Princess Pauahi's legacy.

Ka Mana'o E Pili ana Jā "Lilinoe"
The Composer's Thoughts on "Lilinoe"

"Lilinoe" is a very personal song that I share with the Mokihana Festival in hopes of memorializing this special young woman. She has accomplished so much in her lifetime as a Hula and Tahitian dancer. Her love for hula and the Hawaiian culture never faded, as well as her desire to openly share her cultural knowledge with family, friends, and even strangers. Lilinoe's warm personality allowed all of us to feel of the *mana* (power) that she possessed at such a tender age. She truly was a very gifted young woman who never settled for second best. She was a beautiful child. There was this aura about her—a natural beauty that radiated from within.

All of these recollections and many others are a part of this *mele*—a song that was written to somewhat fill the uneasy void in the lives of her remaining family members and loved ones. But more importantly, this song was composed to remember the comforting promise that families can be together forever through the love of our Heavenly Father.

Ka Wehewehe 'Ana
The Meaning of Each Verse

The entire song was written to convey Lilinoe's life journey—as she moved from Kaua'i (first verse), to O'ahu (second verse), and then to Heaven (third verse).

The first verse expresses the sadness that is felt because of Lilinoe's passing. The allusion to "heavy rains" in Kaua'i's forests symbolizes the *kaona* (underlying meaning) of bitterness and pain. Similarly, the flood-filled forests are the tears of Kaua'i's people, asking Lilinoe to rain peacefully upon them so that they may feel comforted.

The chorus is centered around two Hawaiian values: *aloha* (love) and *mahalo* (gratitude). Remember now that this mist is actually Lilinoe. This fine mist has been guided by the *pueo* (owl) through its journey. The pueo is Lilinoe's 'aumākua, or Hawaiian family god. (Footnote #1 located at the bottom of the lyrics further expounds upon the significance of the pueo). The last line brings closure to the chorus, reemphasizing that families (such as Lilinoe's) can live together forever through love and gratefulness.

The second verse tells of the unconditional love that everyone has for this young woman. In the first verse, the rain fell in Kaua'i, where Lilinoe was born and raised. As we move on to the second verse, we see that the rain has traveled to O'ahu, where Lilinoe's 'ohana currently resides. It is a common trait for Hawaiian composers to commemorate a certain place with the wind name or rain name of that area. The pleasant wind of Kāne'ohe is present in this verse, as it is the home of the Pai family. Once again, the last line repeats itself (from the previous verse), "E Lilinoe i ka lani, e helele'iē"—"Oh heavenly mist, rain down upon us." This was purposely done to express the genuine desire to feel of her ever-gentle presence.

The third verse connects Lilinoe to her ʻohana (family) and hoaloha (friends). These individuals are the lifted "voices" in this paukū. Her older brother's name, *Pihana*, was also added to further unify the concept of Lilinoe's close connection with her loved ones. One of the hōʻailona (signs) for Hawaiians is the rainbow. Although a symbol of serenity and peacefulness, the rainbow (according to Nānā I Ke Kumu) is often associated with death. In this verse, the last line is slightly different, reiterating the significance of the ānuenue (rainbow).

The last verse dedicates this song unto Lilinoe. It identifies sacred places throughout her life—Kāneʻohe, Kauaʻi, and Heaven. The last two lines humbly ask Kumuola, our Heavenly Creator and source of the fine mist, to ensure future growth by letting the rain fall down upon us—or in a figurative sense to allow Lilinoe to always be an important part of our lives.

Lilinoe
Kale Kau'i

Ho'ola'a 'ia no Lilinoe Pai

Lu'ulu'u ka nahele i ka ua nui | The forest is burdened with heavy rains
Helele'i ka ua 'awa o Kaua'i | The bitter rain of Kaua'i falls
'O Kaua'i home o ka lilinoe | Beloved Kaua'i, home of the fine mist
E Lilinoe i ka lani, e helele'i ē | Oh heavenly mist, rain down upon us

HUI:
Aloha nui i ka noe i hele loa | Much love for the mist that has traveled its path
Kia'i 'ia e ka Pueo e hi'ialo | Guarded by the Owl[1] that nurtures and protects
Mahalo nui i ka noe i hele loa | Much thanks for the mist that has traveled its path
M lama 'ia e ka 'ohana e ola mau | Nurtured by a family that will live together forever

He ua ho'oheno 'oe e ku'u noe ē | You are a cherished rain, my endeared mist
Pāmai ka makani 'olu o Kāne'ohe | The wind of Kāne'ohe blows pleasantly
'O Kāne'ohe home o ka lilinoe | Beloved Kāne'ohe, home of the fine mist
E Lilinoe i ka lani, e helele'i ē | Oh heavenly mist, rain down upon us

Hāpai 'ia nāleo iki i ka lani ē | The voices have been lifted to the heavens
Ka home hou o lilinoe pihana i ka la'i | Peace abounds in the new home of this fine mist
I ka la'i pi'i ke ānuenue | In serenity, a rainbow[2] appears
He hō'ailona no ka po'e, e helele'i ē | A reassuring sign for the people, rain down upon us

Eia ku'u leo mele no lilinoe ē | This is my song for the fine mist
O Kāne'ohe, o Kaua'i, o Kumuola | Of Kāne'ohe, of Kaua'i, of our Heavenly Creator
'O Kumuola, kumu o ka lilinoe | Our Maker, source of the fine mist
I ola pono ka honua, e helele'i ē | So that the earth may live, continually rain down upon us

---

[1] The pueo, or owl was often a symbol of guidance. Mary Kawena Pūku'i writes: "the *pueo* causes one to turn back, to take a safe route instead of a dangerous one, to go where help lies. The association goes back to early legends. One tells that the goddess *Hina*, mother of *Māui*, bore another child in the form of the pueo. Later, when *Māui* was taken prisoner and held for sacrifice, the owl rescued him and led him to safety. Another story tells of the beautiful Kahalaopuna. Cruelly beaten by her lover who thought her unfaithful, the maid was left, dead or nearly dead, in a forest. A *pueo* first resuscitated her, then led her to a safe place."

[2] The hō'ailona of the ānuenue (rainbow) is often associated with death.

Both footnotes taken from *Nanā I Ke Kumu (Look to Source)* Volume II, 1972.

After attending the graduation party for Kale Kaui on May 31, 2003, I remained on the island for three days. I was informed about an historic site located along the highway on the road to Poipu and Waimea: the Kilohana Plantation. I went to this site for breakfast and then took a carriage ride around the property. The best way to describe the experience is in pictures: visual images that, in themselves, excite the senses and bring to mind memories of the days of the sugar plantations in the islands.

Carriage in front of Kilohana Plantation

Carriage driver Tony Martin and horse Buddy greet Author Burgess on his second visit to Kilohana in September 2003

The Gardens of the Kilohana Plantation

Another beautiful area of the island is the Nawiliwili Harbor area, the location of two scenic lighthouses: a large lighthouse at the beginning of the entrance to the area; and a second, smaller lighthouse located just off the green of one of the holes of a golf course that overlooks the narrow entrance to the harbor. Having experienced the beauty of the site from the deck of the SS *Independence* on several occasions, I finally had the chance to drive to the shoreline to get a closer look at both lighthouses. The site of the larger building inspired...

The Lighthouse at Nawiliwili Harbor

She stands as a lonely sentinel,
Her beacon as bright as a star,
At the entrance to Nawiliwili Harbor:
Her signal seen clearly from afar.

Waves approach her lava rock fortress
Saluting, as the shoreline they near,
Then crashing in white-capped brilliance
As in thunderous applause they do cheer.

Aircraft approaching Lihue Airport
See the lighthouse beacon as a guide,
Insuring success in their landings.
For her, it's a personal source of pride.

She sends out her greetings of Aloha
To all ships that daily pass by,
Entering and departing from the harbor
'Neath the Kauaian azure blue sky.

The passengers on the ships return the greetings,
Thanking her for guiding the way...
The lighthouse at Nawiliwili Harbor:
A trustworthy friend, night and day.

Driving through the town of Lihue and past the airport, the road turns north toward Kapaa. Watch for the signs that lead to the Wailua River boat dock. The experience of a lifetime awaits: a cruise along the Wailua River to the Fern Grotto, site of many a wedding ceremony on Kauai. You will be serenaded by locals along the way and then awed by the beauty of nature. The trip will be highlighted by the singing of the Hawaiian Wedding Song as you stand in the Grotto. This trip can be best described with photographs (taken during my first visit in December 1995).

Visitors are serenaded during the Wailua River Excursion to the Fern Grotto

The beauty of Wailua River State Park

While on the Wailua River cruise, you will see parts of the Kamokila Hawaiian Village: a replica of one of the ancient Hawaiian villages. Local residents, proud of their ancestral heritage, have established this site so that young Hawaiians, as well as visitors to Kauai, can learn about daily life in the past.

To reach the village, follow the signs to Opaekaa Falls. You will pass the Poliako Heiau on the left, a sacred site of the Hawaiian people that overlooks the Wailua River, and then come to the Falls (on your right). Just pass the Falls is a road that leads off to the left and down to the entrance of the village.

Poliako Heiau

Opaekaa Falls

The Wailua River and the Kamokila Hawaiian Village

Kamokila Hawaiian Village

On a recent trip to Kauai,
In March of two thousand three,
I learned much more
About Hawaiian lore
And about culture and history.

While visiting the site of Opaekaa Falls
I saw a special sign:
"E KOMO MAI",
Please stop by,
Take a walk on a path back in time.

The Kamokila Hawaiian Village
Shows visitors a glimpse of the past.
It allows them to see
The reality
Of a lifestyle that forever will last
In the minds of present-day Hawaiians,
Proud of what their ancestors have done.
This village display
Gives visitors a way
To understand the tapestry that was spun
By early inhabitants of the islands,
Who lived off the land and the sea.
When you come to Kauai,
Take time to stop by:
It's a site that you just have to see!

Kamokila Hawaiian Village

A view toward the Wailua River from the grounds of the Kamokila Hawaiian Village

On each visit to Kauai, I made an effort to learn more about "The Garden Isle" and to see the natural beauty, as well as to observe efforts being made to conserve this natural beauty—thus protecting native wildlife from extinction. A highlight of one trip was a visit to the Kilauea Point National Wildlife Refuge.

This visit inspired a poem about the Refuge and about…

The Lighthouse at Kilauea Point

When I read about a lighthouse on Kauai—
On the island's northernmost point—
I decided to visit this scenic site:
A trip that did not disappoint!
I have seen a number of lighthouses,
For I live near the nation's East Coast
Where lighthouses dot many coastlines,
From Maine to the Florida coast.

As I drove up Highway 56
And was welcomed to Kilauea Point,
My eyes looked around in amazement
At scenes that with pride did anoint
My spirit, as with visions of Nature
My mind and my soul were impressed:
This lighthouse is the site of a refuge
For wildlife, and it's one of the best!

Shearwaters, albatross, and boobies
Are nesting on the rocks by the sea,
Protected from harm by people
Who fight for their right to be free!

Kilauea's lighthouse is indeed a special place
And a model for what can be done
When wildlife is saved from extinction,
NOT viewed through the sight of a gun.

The Kilauea Lighthouse

Views of the Kilauea Point National Wildlife Refuge

After spending the morning at the Kilauea Point National Wildlife Refuge, I continued northeast past the area of Princeville into another Wildlife Refuge in Hanalei. My afternoon was spent exploring...

Hanalei and Beyond

On the Garden Isle of Kauai
Mother Nature puts on a display
Of color, of strength, and of beauty:
Something new lies in store ev'ry day.

As you travel northwest up to Princeville,
The views never cease to impress,
And as you continue your journey,
Your eyes will the landscape caress:

Exploring the white sandy beaches,
Embracing Hanalei Bay;
Hiking the trails of Kalalau,
Investigating caves on the way.

The caves are remains of eruptions—
Tubes through which lava did flow.
As you wander inside them, walk slowly:
Sense their strength and let your mind go.

When you come to the end of your journey,
Hanalei in your thoughts will remain.
The experience you've had has been awesome,
Though not easy in words to explain.

So often we are told that "a picture is worth a thousand words". I believe that and hope the next several pages of photographs taken in the area of Princeville and "Hanalei and Beyond" will reinforce the meaning of this famous statement.

Waterfall at the entrance to the resort area of Princeville

Residences in Princeville area

Palm trees in reflecting pool at the Princeville Hotel Restaurant

Taro patch along the roadside in Hanalei

Sign to Hanalei

One of the spectacular views from a hiking trail near the wet caves near
Hanalei

In the Hanalei area of Kauai, the visitor may stop in for a meal at Tahiti Nui, a quaint restaurant and cocktail lounge located along Route 56. Owner Auntie Louise Marston has been at this spot on Kauai for thirty-five years, and while you are eating, she will come over and "talk story" about her life on the island. (Auntie Louise Marston passed away in September 2003. May this poem—and the photo on page 120—prove to be a fitting tribute to her.)

My experience at Tahiti Nui inspired a poem about…

A Conversation at Tahiti Nui:
Talking Story with Auntie Louise

Tahiti Nui is a Kauaian restaurant
On Route 56 in Hanalei.
It's a quaint place to have a good dinner,
Or to attend a luau on Wednesday.
You also can have breakfast and lunch at this spot,
But what brings many diners here
Are the "best-tasting Mai-Tais" on the island…
And the stories from Auntie Louise they will hear.

When I walked into Tahiti Nui
In the town of Hanalei,
I was hoping to talk with Auntie Louise
While eating some lunch that day.
The conversation that resulted
Kept us talking for nearly two hours:
The topics as varied as alphabet soup,
From soccer to luaus to flowers.

Auntie spoke of the weekends in the sixties
When locals would camp on the beach,
Catching fish with their bamboo poles and their nets:
Fish that were always within reach.
The fish were then cleaned, cooked, and eaten
As the locals would talk story or play.

118

Tourists on the island could not reach this beach
Since the roads were not paved in Hanalei.
Each rainfall turned the roads of dirt
Into mud: quite an obstacle for cars…
The locals could easily walk to the beach
To go fishing and, at night, view the stars.

Many swimmers and surfers have invaded this beach
As the twenty-first century comes to Hanalei:
The fish, once so numerous and easy to catch,
All have been frightened away.

Auntie Louise has been in Hanalei
For more than thirty-five years.
She told me about so many things
That a "mainlander" rarely hears.

Before I left Tahiti Nui that day,
I was given two flower leis:
A gift from owner Auntie Louise Marston,
Who showed kindness in so many ways….

Talking story with a stranger from New Jersey;
Recommending some good foods to eat;
Telling me why she has stayed in Hanalei:
How lucky I was we did meet!

As I drove to the airport that afternoon,
In my thoughts Auntie Louise remained:
A Tahitian lady on the isle of Kauai,
Where the Aloha Spirit still reigns.
The memories I took with me that afternoon
Will be treasures I shall never forget:
In my travels on the Garden Isle of Kauai,
This experience was "as good as it gets"!

Auntie Louise Marston, owner of Tahiti Nui Restaurant in Hanalei, "talks story" with Author Burgess in May 2003

Having experienced Kauai from the ground, I decided to view the island from the air and from the sea: adventures that would focus on the rugged Na Pali Coast along the northwest region—an area very difficult to observe by land. On my May 2003 visit, I drove to the Waimea area and spent the entire day capturing the breathtaking beauty of nature.

My Inter-Island Helicopter adventure in the morning was followed by a late afternoon sunset cruise on board the *Blue Dolphin*. These experiences are described on the next six pages. Following the cruise, I returned to the Radisson Kauai Beach Hotel Resort near the Lihue airport and had a chance to talk with local artist Glenn T. Ichimura (who preferred to call himself a painter). Our conversation resulted in my purchase of one of his paintings of a waterfall on Kauai—AND inspired a poem about how the wonders of nature are captured: by a photographer, by a painter, by a poet.

The adventures begin at the heliport for Inter-Island Helicopters. Fasten your seatbelt, take a deep breath, and enjoy the journey.

One of the most exciting adventures on Kauai is a helicopter ride. I took the challenge of signing up for a tour with Inter-Island Helicopters—a tour in a helicopter WITHOUT DOORS. The flight inspired...

A Helicopter Flight through Paradise on the Garden Isle of Kauai

I flew with Inter-Island Helicopters,
Departing from Port Allen on Kauai,
In a vehicle with no doors to hinder
Displays of Nature seen from on high.

Hidden beyond the sentinels of Na Pali
In the valleys so lush and pristine
Are breathtaking views of beauty
That only from above can be seen...

Magnificent waterfalls cascading
Down cliffs—from sources unknown—
Surrounded by plants and by flowers
That by birds in flight have been sown.

The lava rock peaks have been covered
By grasses, mosses, and ferns:
Decorations provided by rainfall
Falling daily to the dance of the terns.

As the helicopter circles through the valleys,
Hovering near sites rarely seen,
The real hidden treasures on the island of Kauai
Engrave images on the mind's memory screen:

Images of indescribable beauty
In landscapes untouched by mankind,
Proudly displayed by the Creator
In this Paradise that is one of a kind.

Aerial views of Na Pali Coast of Kauai taken on Inter-Island Helicopter
Trip

Aerial view of Waimea Canyon

The rugged landscape on the Na Pali section of Kauai

The Rugged Na Pali Coastline

On the Garden Isle of Kauai
The Na Pali Coastline displays
The works of Mother Nature and Madame Pele:
Waterfalls and lava caves that portray
Elements of the history of the island
And aspects of beauty beyond words;
Hiking trails bordered by tropical flowers,
The homeland of many island birds
That feed in the rugged environment,
Along with some wild mountain goats.
Visitors can view all this beauty
From the decks of a variety of boats.

The weather changes rapidly along Na Pali,
With showers and squalls often seen,
Followed by magnificent rainbows
That add color to the browns and the greens.

The rainbows appear near the shoreline,
Then silently rise through the air,
Framed by the cliffs of Na Pali:
What a thrill for all those who are there!

From the waters along the coast of Na Pali,
Hikers can often be seen
On the cliffs that stand guard o'er the shoreline:
Silent sentinels dressed proudly in green.

The hikers may spend several hours
Reaching some great lookout site,
Then, before returning to the real world,
Camping out on the cliffs for a night.

Views along the Na Pali Coast of Kauai from the deck of the *Blue Dolphin*

The Na Pali Coast of Kauai

Poolside at the Radisson Kauai Beach Resort

Torch Lighting Ceremony in progress (center) at sunset at the Radisson Kauai Beach Resort

Five Sisters' Falls near Na Pali Coast

Painter Glenn Ichimura shows one of his works at the gallery on the grounds of the Radisson Kauai Beach Resort

The Photographer, the Painter, and the Poet

A photographer, a painter, and a poet
Met on the isle of Kauai.
Each one had a goal:
That of touching the soul
Of those who are anxious to see
The beauty of a Garden Isle waterfall
That entertains the birds, plants, and flowers,
Cascading from on high
As birds, drawing nigh,
Circle 'round the white water tower.

The photographer sets up his tripod,
Then mounts his camera in place:
His photograph shows
How the waterfall flows
Past the birds that its moisture embrace.
The photographer captures some trees and some flowers
That are growing in this idyllic spot…
Their shapes are not clear,
For little sunlight appears,
Thus the waterfall dominates the shot.

The painter sits in silence for hours,
His senses soaking in sights and sounds:
Images of life
Filled with joy, mixed with strife,
Then puts onto his canvas what he's found.
Flowers and plants watch the waterfall,
As an audience watches actors on a stage;
Nearby trees seem enthralled;
Lava rocks seem appalled,
Perhaps they're just showing their age.

The poet is excited about what he feels
As he listens to the water and to the birds.
Yet he lacks visual cues
That his readers can use:
His images must be created with words.

131

He tells how the waterfall brings flowers to life,
Causing them in brilliance to bloom...
But also reveals,
How the waterfall feels,
Trying to penetrate the darkness and gloom.

In March of 2003, Wesley Kaui told me that he, Haunani, and Cousin Joyce
would be appearing at a luau as the entertainers. I stopped by and experienced...

A Special Musical Performance by Friends I've Met on Kauai

I came to a Friday night luau
At the Princeville, Kauai, hotel
To be entertained by some Kauaian friends:
Local residents whom I knew quite well.
One performer was Haunani Kaui,
A second was Cousin Joyce,
The third was Sergeant Wesley:
Who supplied the group's tenor voice.
The ukulele was played by Cousin Joyce,
With bass fiddle rhythms by Haunani,
The guitar was played by Police Sergeant Wesley:
A very talented trio on Kauai.

They performed in English and in Hawaiian
For the special event held that night.
The beauty of the melodies
Was a source of rhythmic delight.

Another friend was part of the program:
Kumu Kapu Kinimaka with her hula halau.
The young Hawaiians performed with precision,
Entertaining the guests at the luau...
A trio of talented musicians
And dancers from the isle of Kauai:
Reflections of artistic beauty
In the tropical islands of Hawaii.

Haunani is the kumu who entertained on board the SS *Independence* until the cruise line declared bankruptcy in late 2001. Although I didn't realize it then, I have learned that Haunani, whose last name is Kaui, is related to the Kaui family. (What a small world!)

Haunani currently entertains diners who come to the Hula Girl Restaurant in the Coconut Marketplace Shopping Center in Kapaa. Cousin Haunani, along with Cousin Keala Senkus, performs several nights a week at this local restaurant.

On one of my visits to Kauai, Kawika Kaui—the young hula dancer who became the mascot of the SS *Independence*—invited me to his school to share some of my poetry with his classmates. His class presented me a handmade lei and his father, Sergeant Wesley Kaui of the Hanalei Police Department at the time, took me on a guided tour of the school. Sergeant Kaui then invited me to go on his "rounds" and presented me a t-shirt, making me an honorary member of the Kauai Police Force. When I left Kauai later that week, Wesley, his wife Trinette, and son Kawika came to the airport to wish me well and to present me a flower lei. Their older son Kale was at the Kamehameha School in Honolulu at the time. Kawika is now enrolled at this school on the island of Oahu. As is often said, "a picture is worth a thousand words"… and the following photos reflect some great memories.

Sergeant Wesley Kaui on duty in Hanalei in 1998

Wesley, Trinette, and son David present Author Burgess a flower lei and
extend farewell Aloha wishes at the Lihue airport in 1998

I conclude my tour of "The Garden Isle" with several images of the natural beauty of the island, from incredible double rainbows to the magnificence of a Kauai sunset.

A beautiful double rainbow appears along the beach of the Coconut Palm Resort near Kapaa

The Little Lighthouse at Nawiliwili Harbor adjacent to a golf course

Natural beauty on the grounds of the Kilohana Plantation

Sunset near Waimea

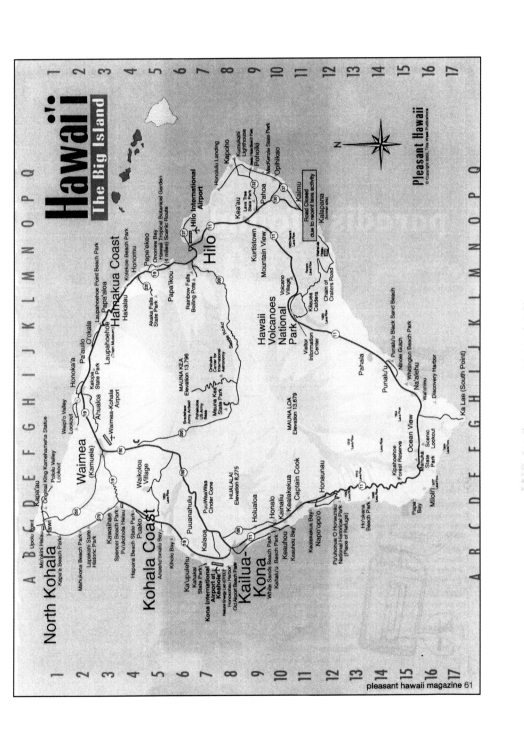

Hawai'i
The Big Island

Pleasant Hawaii
© Copyright 2002, The Hysan Publications

Hawaii

*W*henever someone hears a reference to "The Big Island", images of Mauna Kea, the volcanic mountains, come to mind, along with stories about the coffee plantations, the cattle ranches, and the locations famous for displays of orchids. However, there is much more to the beauty of the island of Hawaii.

On one of my island cruises, in April of 1998, I had the opportunity to witness the grace and the skill of hula performers from around the state as they participated in the Annual Merry Monarch Festival. After watching some of the groups perform, I took a self-guided walking tour through the Liliuokalani Gardens and came across a charming site known as Moku Ola. As always, my timing seemed to be perfect and I had the chance to chat with a group of children from a local elementary school: the Hale Aloha Nazarene School. The students had come to the area for lunch with their teachers, one of whom was Mrs. Endriss. I requested permission to take a photo of the students, dressed in their school uniforms. (When I returned to the Mainland, I sent copies of the photo to the school, along with a letter, thanking the teachers and the students for extending the "Spirit of Aloha" to a visitor and educator from the Mainland.)

Allow me to share with you some of the photos I took on that special April afternoon....

After returning to the SS *Independence* that afternoon, I spoke with the ship's kumu, Haunani Kaui, about my experience and then went to my cabin and composed a poem about...

Moku Ola: Hilo, Hawaii

The cruise ship SS *Independence*
Docked in Hilo this morning at eight.
After breakfast on board,
My spirit then soared
As new adventures my eyes did await.

I entered Liliuokalani Gardens,
Located along Banyon Drive.
I sat for a while
Taking in, with a smile,
Nature's beauty, so picturesque and alive.

I later walked over a footbridge
To Moku Ola, an island retreat,
The palm trees waved hi
As the Tradewinds passed by...
While the waves softly lapped at my feet.

A group of young children soon joined me.
(They had gathered, with their teachers, for lunch.)
They all seemed so proud
As they shouted aloud—
While on some great snacks they did munch—
"Thank you for coming to Hilo
And for stopping to sit for a while!
We're certain you see
What fills us with glee."
My spirit was touched by their smile.

"Aloha", I said to the children.
"Mahalo for sharing that smile.
You've indeed made my day:
I wish I could stay
And talk with you all for a while."

As I started my walk back to the dockside,
I thanked God for this so special day...
And somehow I know
That although I must go,
I'll come back to Moku Ola someday.

When I spoke with kumu Haunani
At tea time this afternoon,
She told me much more
Of this place I adore—
And to which I'll return someday soon.
She explained that the site Moku Ola
Is known as a calm "healing place".
Locals swim to this isle
To rest for a while
So the gods can restore them with grace.

Today the site offers a setting
That inspires all those who stop by:
As they sit by the sea,
Their spirits are set free,
Gently floating in the blue Hilo sky.

I traveled by bus to the incredible Volcano National Park on the Big Island and witnessed some of the great power that has been shown by the volcanic eruptions on the island. On one occasion, I took a helicopter flight over the volcanos and saw the lava descending toward the ocean. The following images were captured during the trips....

Steam clouds rising from the south shore of Hawaii as lava enters the water. Photos taken on April 2, 1998.

In the history of the islands, Madame Pele is a famous, well-respected, and honored figure. She is the Fire Goddess who resides in the Halemaumau Crater on the island of Hawaii. Her power and her strength can be seen in the areas on the island where lava flows have covered roadways and beaches; her beauty can be seen in the ongoing display of lava entering the waters on the south side of the island, sending billows of steam clouds into the air while adding new land to the island.

Madame Pele: painted by Artist-Historian Herb Kawainui Kane

This painting by Artist Herb Kane shows the goddess Pele in one of her many forms. As mentioned above, her traditional home is the active crater Halemaumau at the Kilauea Volcano on the island of Hawaii.

On my first cruise through the islands, in December of 1996, I was witness to the incredible power and beauty of Madame Pele as the SS *Independence* sailed past the southern tip of the island at night. The crew of the ship held a ceremony, thanking the Fire Goddess for providing the visitors a memorable moment on the cruise. As part of the ceremony, the crew performed a special hula and recited a chant, honoring Madame Pele. I was inspired to compose a poem about what I witnessed that evening. I showed the poem to the ship's kumu, Kahea Beckley, and was both surprised and honored when he asked me to read the poem to all of the passengers during the final program on the cruise.

On my second cruise, in April of 1998, the same kumu was on board and he asked me to participate in the ceremony on Thursday evening... by reading my entire poetic tribute to Madame Pele. WOW! What a special moment in my poetic career. On board the ship that week was a hula instructor from the island of Kauai. After the ceremony ended, she approached and asked for a copy of my poem. She said she would like to make an effort to translate the poem into the Hawaiian language and then use the story as the basis for a new hula dance. She said she could already envision the motions that could be included in the hula.

To say that I was speechless would be the understatement of the century. It was such an honor knowing that a local Hawaiian resident felt I had captured something special in my poem.

I hope you will enjoy reading the images I included in my...

Tribute to Madame Pele

The cloud-like curtains had parted
In the skies o'er the isle of Hawaii
As the audience awaited in silence
An event taking place on the isle.

The celestial spotlight was shining
On the stage near Hawaii's south shore
As kumu Kahea introduced us—
In his Hawaiian narrative style—
To the wondrous performance of Madame Pele,
The Fire Goddess of Halemaumau.

From underground tunnels and pathways
That descend from the famed Kilauea
Appeared, in a fiery production,
Molten lava that danced on the shores,
Then entered the waters with charisma,
Sending steam clouds in the shape of Protea
Billowing into the heavens,
Whirling in the light of the moon,
While the lava added land to the island
In an act of creation unique.

The audience paid tribute to Madame Pele
While the kumu praised her work in a chant,
And we all were inspired by her beauty...
And awed by her strength and mistique.

Poet Burgess reads his "Tribute to Madame Pele" as part of the ceremony on board the SS *Independence* in honor of the Fire Goddess

During a visit to Maui in February of 2003, I was told of an annual cultural-festival on the Big Island that is held in August at the Pu'ukoholā Heiau National Historic Site. The day begins at 7:00 A.M. with the Na Papa Kanaka o Pu'ukoholā Heiau (Royal Court Procession), followed by the Ho'okupu (Gift Giving Rituals) and some reenactments by Court Dancers. I was invited to attend this ceremony, held at the Pu'ukoholā Heiau (Temple on the Hill of the Whale), in Kawaihae.

This temple was built by Kamehameha I in 1790-1791. History tells the story of how the temple came into existence; the prophet Kapoukahi told the aunt of Kamehameha I that he (Kamehameha) would conquer all the islands of Hawaii if he built a large heiau dedicated to his family war god Kuka'ilimoku (Ku) atop Pu'ukoholā —"Hill of the Whale"—at Kawaihae. The heiau (temple) measures 224 by 100 feet, with walls 16 to 20 feet high on the landward side and on the ends. At the time, its platform was crowded with ceremonial structures. Today it is the location of cultural events.

I accepted the invitation and attended the Saturday, August 16, 2003, ceremony, arriving at 5:00 A.M. in order to observe the preparations for the Royal Court Procession and to speak with several of the participants in this two-hour cultural event. It is a morning that will live in my memory forever. One of the things that proved very interesting to me was that part of the ceremonial dress of Kamehameha included a whale tooth pendant carved in the shape of a tongue, symbolic of "one who speaks with authority".

I present a photographic glimpse of this ceremony, showing the heiau, the lele (tower on which the gift offerings were placed), a reenactment of a ritual by the Court Dancers, and the departure from the ceremonial area by the participants.

I also revisited a site I had seen during my 1998 cruise: the Pu'uhonua o Hōnaunau (Place of Refuge) along the Kona Coast of the Island. This site preserves aspects of traditional Hawaiian life.

Hōnaunau Bay was a natural place for the ali'i (Royal Chiefs) to establish one of their most important residences. Separated from the royal grounds by a massive wall was the pu'uhonua, a place of refuge for those who violated the Kapu, the sacred laws. The pu'uhonua was a sanctuary that provided a second chance to those violators. If successful in reaching a "place of refuge", a ceremony of absolution was performed by the kahuna pule (priest). The offender could then return home safely.

The photos seen here are: the Keone'ele, the cove used as a royal canoe landing and forbidden to all commoners; the Ki'i (wooden images) that stand watch over the reconstruction of a temple and mausoleum, which housed the bones of 23 ali'i; and the temple, showing the lele (tower) on which the Ho'okupu (offerings) were placed.

The Temple on the Hill of the Whale in Kawaihae

The Lele of the Pu'ukoholā Heiau in Kawaihae

Participants in the ceremony on the Hill of the Whale in a reenactment of exercises of strength

Scene at the end of the ceremony, showing Kamehameha and his followers departing the grounds of the Heiau in Kawaihae

Have you ever dreamed of riding off into the sunset on one of the oldest and largest cattle ranches in America? For this author, that dream came true while on a visit to the 175,000-acre Parker Ranch, on the Big Island. One of the owners of Cowboys of Hawaii at Parker Ranch, Karoll Penovaroff, took me on an unforgettable two-hour riding experience that allowed me to learn about the life of the Paniolos (the Hawaiian Cowboys). Penovaroff was accompanied by a young student, Braiden Malicki, who hopes to work full time on the Parker Ranch someday. As a career Spanish instructor, knowing that the word "paniolo" comes from the Spanish word "español", I like to refer to the experience as...

The Day I Became a Paniolo

It began with an early wakeup call—
At 5:15 in the morning.
After a shower,
I drove for an hour,
On the Parker Ranch to go exploring.

My adventure was completed on horseback,
On a steed with the name Butter Ball:
He would walk, and then trot,
But I ne'er got upsot!
(That is, from the horse, I never did fall.)

It was only my second time on horseback.
(Haleakala, Maui, was the first.)
This time I was glad
That I knew what to pad
So no blood vessels on my "seat" would burst.

The Parker Ranch ride was exciting
And it gave me a peek at the world
Of the Hawaiian cowboy,
Who lived life with much joy,
While enduring many hardships, which at him were hurled.

The weather conditions on the 175,000-acre ranch
Are often unfavorable, at best.
Yet the paniolo survives,
Although often deprived
Of the "comforts of home" as he faces each new test.

This way of life continues to challenge all those
Who love riding the range each day...
And on one August morn
Their lifestyle was worn
By a writer from New Jersey who into their world did stray.

Author Burgess and horse Butter Ball, ready to ride the range at Parker Ranch

Karoll Penovaroff gives her horse a break at a water trough during the ride on the Parker Ranch

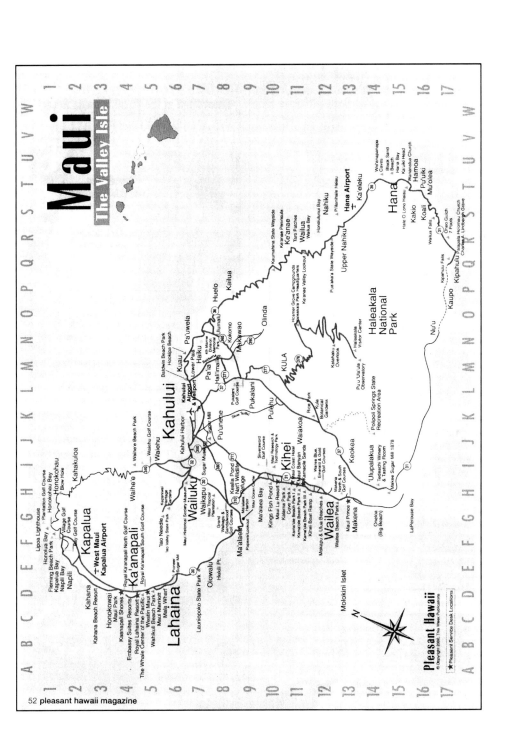

Maui
The Valley Isle

Kapalua
West Maui
Kapalua Airport
Ka'anapali
Lahaina
Wailuku
Kahului
Kahului Airport
Waikapu
Ma'alaea
Wailea
Makena
Kihei
Waiakoa
KULA
Pukalani
Makawao
Haiku
Pa'ia
Pa'uwela
Huelo
Kailua
Ke'anae
Nahiku
Upper Nahiku
Hana Airport
Hana
Haleakala National Park
Kaupo
Nu'u

Lipoa Lighthouse
Honolua Bay
Plantation Golf Course
Honokohau Bay
Blow Hole
Fleming Beach Park
Kapalua Bay
Napili Bay
Napili
Village Golf Course
Bay Golf Course
Kahakuloa
Kahana
Kahana Beach Resort
Honokowai
Maui Park
Kaanapali Shores
Royal Ka'anapali North Golf Course
Embassy Suites Resorts
Royal Lahaina Resort
Westin Maui
The Whale Center of the Pacific
Wahikuli Beach Park
Maui Marriott
Mala Wharf
Royal Ka'anapali South Golf Course
Waihe'e
Waihe'e Beach Park
Waiehu Golf Course
Waiehu
Kahului Harbor
Pioneer Sugar Mill
'Iao Needle
'Iao Valley State Park
Kepaniwai Heritage Gardens
Maui Historical Society Museum
Sugar Mill
Sugar Mill
Puunene
Olowalu
Launiupoko State Park
Heikii Pt.
Maui Tropical Plantation
Grand Wailea & Sandblood Golf Courses
Papawai Lookout
Maui Ocean Center
Maui Lu Resort
Kealia Park
Ma'alaea Harbor
Kamaole Beach Park I
Kamaole Beach Park III
Kihei Boat Ramp
Kealia Pond Nat'l Wildlife Refuge
Kings Fish Pond
Maui Banyan
Maui Coast Hotel
Kamaole Sands
Wailea North & South Golf Courses
Mokapu & Ulua Beaches
Wailea Beach Park
Maui Prince
Oneloa (Big Beach)
LaPerouse Bay
Makena North & South Golf Courses
Silversword Golf Course
Maui Research & Technology Park
Waine Blue, Emerald & Gold Golf Courses
Kula Botanical Gardens
Rice Park
Pukalani Golf Course
Hali'imaile
Kahakuloa Overlook
Kula
Keokea
Silent Traffic
'Ulupalakua
Tedeschi Winery & Tasting Room
Makee Sugar Mill 1878
Polipoli Springs State Recreation Area
Puu 'Ula'ula Observatory
Haleakala Visitor Center
Kokomo
Olinda
Lower Paia
Hookipa Beach
Baldwin Beach Park
Kuau
4th Marine Division Memorial Park
Kaumahina State Wayside
Ke'anae Peninsula
Taro Patches
Ke'anae Valley Lookout
Wailua
Wailua Bay
Honolulunui Bay
Puaa'kaa State Wayside
Pi'ilanihale Heiau
Ka'eleku
Hana Bay
Wananalua Church
Hamoa
Mu'olea
Pu'uiki
Koali
Kakio
Hale O Lono Heiau
Wailua Falls
Kipahulu
Kipahulu
Palapala Ho'omau Church
Charles A. Lindbergh Grave
'Ohe'o Gulch
7 Pools
Kipahulu Falls
Wai'anapanapa Caves
Black Sand Beach
Hana Bay
Ka'uiki Head

Molokini Islet
N

Pleasant Hawaii
© Copyright 2000, The Week Publications
★ Pleasant Service Desk Locations

Maui

7he final destination on my "Fleeting Glimpse of Paradise" is Maui: my island home. I begin with a poem I composed in 1999, reflecting the motto for the island: "Maui is the best" in the Hawaiian language...

Maui No Ka Oi

The rustling of the palm fronds,
Conversing with the breeze;
The chirping of the native birds,
Constructing nests with ease;
The pounding of the white capped waves,
Announcing that they're near;
The straining of the small boat's sails,
Caressing air so clear;
The puffing up of snow-white clouds,
Performing in the skies;
The breaching of the humpback whales,
Showcasing their great size;
The dancing of the sugar cane,
Whispering in the fields;
The blooming of plumeria,
Revealing what nature yields;
The calling of the gecko,
Scampering 'cross the wall;
The croaking of an island frog,
Awaiting a playmate's call.

These are images one will see
On Maui, "The Valley Isle":
Without a doubt, NO KA OI,
Guaranteed to produce a smile.

In a previous poem, written during a visit in 1998—also entitled "Maui No Ka Oi"—I provided a brief description for various locations on the island. That poem began with the lines...

The visitor to Maui
Will find it hard to leave;
The weather's great;
The food, first-rate;
Scenic views one can't believe.
Each section of the island
Has much for one to see,
From sacred pools
To coral jewels
That sparkle brilliantly.

The question is, where to begin the tour? I decided to begin at what appears on a map to be the "forehead" of the island, in the areas of Kapalua (an area that has a butterfly as its symbol!), Napili, and Kahana. From there I shall take you through the Kaanapali area into the quaint town of Lahaina, located on the west side of the West Maui Mountains. Next, it's on to the area of Maalaea and the Maui Ocean Center. Following a brief stop at the Maui Tropical Plantation, I'll take you to Wailuku, to Kahului (the spot where most tourists arrive by plane on their visit), and then on to Paia, to Kuau (famous for its windsurfing beach), and then onto the road to Hana and the final resting place of aviator Charles Lindbergh. Returning to Kahului, the tour will go to Makawao and into Upcountry Maui, with the final destination being Haleakala National Park, with its Silversword plants and the awesome beauty of the volcanic cinder cones, seen from an altitude of 10,002 feet above sea level—the highest point on Maui. Descending from Haleakala, my tour will end with visits to Kihei, Wailea, and Makena. Along the way, I shall show you the natural beauty of Maui, some fascinating destinations and, of course, a personal look at some of the residents who provided the inspiration for this collection of poems and photographs.

The first glimpse will be of...

Kahana and Napili
And Kapalua, too
They provide each guest
Idyllic rest:
Each day brings something new.

I have chosen the image of a butterfly, on display in Kapalua in December of 1998. It is the symbol of this area of the island.

In December of 1998, I came to Maui for a five-week stay that began with a week at the…

Papakea Resort in Honokōwai:
The Land of Rainbows

The memories of my one-week stay
At the Papakea Resort
Are highlighted by the rainbows
Of every size and sort.
They greeted me at breakfast;
They came and went all day:
Full rainbows over land and sea,
So brilliantly on display.
One traveled o'er the horizon,
First anchored out at sea...
Then moving slowly inward
To the beach quite close to me.
From my oceanfront apartment—
Apartment F–110—
The rainbows danced before me,
Delighting me—and then—
Disappearing silently,
Into a sky of blue….
Then returning for a quick encore
Before their play was through.
These natural phenomena,
Like paintings in the sky
Created by our Saviour's brush
In HIS studio on High,
Stand out among my memories
Like jewels upon a crown:
Highlights of my visit
Near quaint Lahaina town.

Lahaina offers everyone
A glimpse of times gone by,
When whaling ships
Made frequent trips
The humpback whales to spy.

Lahaina served as the whaling village during the nineteenth century. Today the visitor can see many historical sites and displays that bring to life those whaling days. Of course, modern-day Lahaina offers the visitor many other experiences—from the world's largest banyan tree to the galleries of some of the world's finest artists and artisans to a ride on the sugarcane train to a variety of fine shops and restaurants.

Bubba Gump's, located along Front Street, has a bench outside that was used in the movie *Forrest Gump*. The restaurant management gave me permission to use this bench as my starting point in my "Fleeting Glimpse of Paradise". I begin my photo collage of Lahaina at Bubba Gump's....

The whaling ship *The Carthaginian* in Lahaina

Dolphin Topiary along Front Street in Lahaina

The largest banyan tree in the world sits in Lahaina across the street from the Pioneer Inn

Sand artist in Lahaina working on a new image

The piece of sand art, framed and on display during a Friday night exhibition in Lahaina

One activity on every visitor's itinerary during a visit to the island of Maui should be that of...

A Friday Night in Lahaina

I drove into Lahaina town
One Friday afternoon.
I witnessed three bright rainbows
And then, a bright full moon.
I sat beneath the banyan tree
And gazed on out to sea,
Inspired by the sunset
Taking place in front of me.
I took a dozen photographs
To help recall the scenes:
The artists and the fishermen;
The gorgeous blues and greens.

And when the sun had gone from view,
I strolled along Front Street
Until I got to BJ'S
Where I went upstairs to eat.
I dined in scenic splendor,
With sites that are well known:
The stately Carthaginian,
Whose sails Tradewinds have blown;
The Wharf, from ancient whaling days,
Now filled with art displays;
The many stores on Front Street
Where tourists come to gaze.

I then took time to watch in awe
Some artists from the isle
As they performed their magic
In unique Hawaiian style;
Creations made with grains of sand
Within a frame of glass;
The paintings of the humpback whales
Which none will e'er surpass;

The art of Christian Lassen
And the Wyland magic touch
That make the ocean come alive,
While teaching us so much!

And if you like to listen
To songs and poetry,
Tropic Provisions Bookstore
Is just the place to be...
For local island talent
Is showcased there each night
From seven until ten P.M.—
'Tis an artist's true delight!

Lahaina is a special place,
Of that there is no doubt.
So, when YOU come to Maui,
Stop by and check it out.

This is another poem that was composed in December of 1994. The Tropic Provisions Bookstore no longer exists in its quaint setting in town, but there are many other spots where the poet or music lover can spend several hours of enjoyment. Just ask any local resident for information. After all, that's how *I* found out where to go.

I finish my tour of Lahaina and of this section of west Maui with several more visual images—several thousand more photographic "words" for your viewing enjoyment....

MacGregor's Point on the road to Lahaina

Sunset from the lookout point along the road to Lahaina

A new visitor attraction was opened in the spring of 1998: a site that provides local residents and tourists opportunities to experience the world in the seas that surround the Hawaiian Islands. This unique educational destination on Maui is...

The Maui Ocean Center:
A Project Completed with Pride

Some people would say that Friday the Thirteenth
Is very unlucky, indeed...
And, when it coincides with a brilliant full moon,
There's no doubt that we all must take heed.
(Tho' this may be so,
I want you to know
That exceptions appear
Which make us all cheer!)

Because...

'Twas Friday, March 13, on the calendar
And the full moon welcomed in a great day
In nineteen hundred ninety-eight
Along the shores of Ma'alaea Bay.
That morning, on the island of Maui,
Many residents were shouting: "HOORAY!"
For the exciting new Maui Ocean Center
Opened its doors to the public that day.

As a special event for the opening,
A special friend of the sea—whom we know—
Was present to inspire the visitors:
His name is Jean-Michel Cousteau.
Jean-Michel told us WHY we must care about
Protecting our friends in the sea,
Discussing the role of sea creatures...
And how they protect you and me.

When you visit the Maui Ocean Center,
Take your time and enjoy what you'll see:
Find out why men like Jean-Michel Cousteau
Spend their lives studying Earth's great living sea.

Visit the Ocean Center's large living reef
To see just how alive reefs can be;
Then walk on over to the turtle lagoon
Where Hawaii's green turtles you'll see;
Take some time to investigate the touch pool,
Where urchins and starfish await;
Then stroll on over to stingray cove
To touch the "wings" of the rays. (Don't hesitate!)
Now enter the Whale Discovery Center
To learn more about Maui's humpback whales;
Then go on the underwater journey
Where you'll watch fish with all types of tails
As they swim by in breathtaking patterns—
Coexisting in their undersea realm—
Allowing you to learn of their lifestyles,
Which your senses will, of course, overwhelm.

You will learn a great deal about sea life
That exists in our oceans today;
About life in the reefs made of coral
And the fish that within them do stay;
About ways in which WE can make certain
That life in the seas will survive
So that children growing up in the future
Will continue to enjoy viewing—LIVE—
The wonderful world of our oceans,
Made cleaner and safer each day
By OUR efforts to assist Mother Nature
To preserve what we're observing today.

After you visit this new center
And observe what goes on 'neath the waves,
Don't forget about what you've learned from this visit!
(And why about it everyone raves!)

Do YOUR part to protect the sea creatures!
It's a challenge that we all have to share.
Don't pollute when you're out in the water:
Show the sea creatures that you REALLY care.

Jean-Michel Cousteau at Maui Ocean Center, March 13, 1998

I visited the Maui Ocean Center again on February 12, 2001, spending nearly seven hours exploring the various areas of the complex. Ninety minutes of the visit were spent observing the inhabitants of....

The Jellyfish World

Pulsating in the currents,
Jellyfish move with ease
Like miniature papier-mâché spacecraft
Being carried by a breeze.

Made of ninety-percent water,
Shimmering in the light,
They float like watery mushrooms,
Then disappear from sight...
Descending through the currents
Like kites in the air, flying high,
Propelled by mysterious motors—
Intriguing to the human eye.

In the Maui Ocean Center
They have their own display.
As we come to their exhibit,
They, like palm fronds in the Tradewinds, sway,
Keeping all of us mesmerized
As we sit and watch them in flight:
The beautiful translucent jellyfish
In their world of visual delight.

I was glad to know I had remembered that rule followed by all writers: Never go anywhere without pen and paper. After all, you never know when inspiration will "hit" you. This poem was composed while I sat observing the movements of the jellyfish in the special exhibit at the center. I took the photo that appears on the next page... as a reminder of the experience.

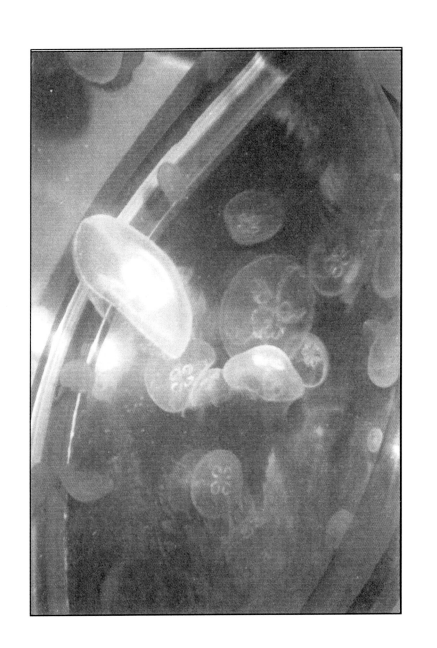

When the visitor leaves the Ma'alaea Harbor area, four possible roads can be followed—leading to Kihei, to Wailea, to Kahului, and to Wailuku, where government offices are located. I shall take you now to Wailuku, stopping for a photographic tour of the Maui Tropical Plantation. This visitor destination provides opportunities to learn more about the agricultural wealth of the island, with exhibits and an educational train ride that explores the many crops that are grown on the islands. The complex also includes a gift shop and a restaurant. Here are several views of what you will see....

As the visitor travels to Wailuku from the Maui Tropical Plantation, he or she will have some fabulous views of the Kahului area and the airport. Arriving in Wailuku, follow the sign that leads to the Iao Valley, the site of one of the most recognized landmarks on the island: the Iao Needle. This area is filled with history and culture and has a museum, a number of hiking trails and picnic areas, and awesome views of the natural phenomenon, the Iao Needle. Along the road that leads to the parking lot is a valley surrounded by hills. On the rock wall of one of the hills is what appears to be the profile of John F. Kennedy. I'll take you on a brief photographic excursion of this site.

The scenic Iao Valley
Reflects the culture's past.
The tales of war,
And much, much more,
Bring mem'ries that will last.

After leaving the Iao Valley, Kaahumanu Avenue takes you into the city of Kahului. In this section of the island, one sees the port, several shopping centers, two high schools, the Maui Community College, the Maui Arts and Cultural Center, and the major airport. As a career educator, I always seem to find myself "pulled toward" schools during my visits. On several occasions, I have offered to share some of my poetry with students in schools of all grade levels.

During my stay on Maui in 2001, I was invited to share some of my poetry with the students at Maui High School and at Baldwin High School. While visiting Baldwin High School, I decided to stroll around the campus during a break between sessions. On my stroll, I came across one building that had a beautiful mural that had been designed and created by the art students of the school. My curiosity resulted in an incredible learning experience. I begin with a photo of the mural....

As I came closer to the mural, I saw an inscription in the building wall, describing the mural....

NA WAI A'O ANA O BALDWIN
(THE TEACHING WATERS OF BALDWIN)
July, 2000

Water is a life source. It flows and travels freely, picking things up along the way, leaving its mark where it has been.

In this mural, the water symbolizes the passing of knowledge between generations of students and teachers. Wakea is the Sky Father, the source of knowledge and water. Papa Hanau Moku is the Mother Earth, the source of land, a filter of knowledge. Hands reach out for knowledge, hands pass knowledge on. The cycle continues.

How lucky can an educator from the Mainland get! Below the inscription was a list of contributors and artists, with a special note of "Mahalo" for assistance. I would be remiss if I did not include the names of these contributors....

Kirk Kurokawa	Elijah Cabiles	Wallace Kuloloio
Anna Duvall	Marween Yagin	Gary Suter
Alexis Dixon	Karla Nakashima	Grace Taguchi
Jen Toba	Noble Richardson	Wallace Fujii
Elmer Bio, Jr.	Tod Gushiken	Janet Sato
Scott Hinau	Wade Hondo	

After copying the inscription, I took several closeup photos of the three main panels in the mural: Wakea, Papa Hanau Moku, the Student. The taro plant is shown in the mural—one of the plants on the islands that grow in water. The next three pages show the extraordinary talents of the students in the art classes who created the mural....

Papa Hanau Moku, Mother Earth

The Student, receiving knowledge from the Sky Father, the Mother Earth and, in the present, from Teachers

Wakea, the Sky Father

When I returned to the main office at the school, I asked about the incredible mural and was told I could learn more by speaking with Janet Sato, the art teacher at Baldwin. She explained that, as was indicated in the inscription, water symbolizes the passing of knowledge; it represents the opportunity to absorb knowledge (just as the taro plant absorbs water to survive and grow). Life is knowledge and, as depicted in the mural, teachers are "life", providing knowledge to the youth. The knowledge is there, but the youth must reach out for it in order to grow. WOW! What an image!

Ms. Sato then told me a little about the history of the land in the section of the island surrounding Baldwin High School. It is the "land of the four waters". In Hawaiian, the word for water is "wai". The four towns located around Baldwin High School are named Waiehu, Waihe'e, Waikapu, and Wailuku. She then said I might be interested in talking with Wallace Kuloloio. Mr. Kuloloio is Hawaiian, and the students asked him to serve as the model for the depiction of Wakea, the Sky Father, in the mural. Mr. Kuloloio is a member of the maintenance staff at Baldwin High.

I searched for this very proud individual on campus, found him, spoke with him about his life on the island, and then requested permission to take several photographs so that I could show my teaching colleagues on the Mainland this special resident who was chosen by the students to represent Sky Father in the mural.

Mahalo nui loa to Ms. Sato, who helped me understand "the story behind the images" in the mural.

Janet Sato, Art Instructor at Baldwin High School

My hometown of Audubon, New Jersey, is becoming known as the "Most Patriotic Small Town in America"—the result of the patriotic achievements of the students in the Audubon public schools. These achievements inspired me to write the book *The Green Wave and the Navy: The History of the USS Benfold* (DDG-65). The ship is a destroyer in the US Pacific Fleet named for one of Audubon's THREE Medal of Honor recipients. A patriotic documentary film has been produced from the book—a film focusing on the work of the young citizens in Audubon.

While at Baldwin High School in September of 2001, I was encouraged to make contact with the JROTC instructor on campus, CSM (Command Sergeant Major) Peter E. Pacyao, a veteran of twenty-seven years of military service. CSM Pacyao most recently had served in Desert Storm and in the area of Kosovo-Herzegovina. When CSM Pacyao heard about my work (I was donating a copy of the book to the school's library and had shown him the copy) and then learned about the successful naval career of my co-author, Chief Petty Officer Danny K. Edgar, he invited me to speak to his classes during my upcoming visit to Maui in February 2002. The experience was one of the most rewarding in my educational career, and it inspired a poetic salute to...

Sergeant Major Peter E. Pacyao:
An American Hero at Baldwin High School

After twenty-seven years in the service,
Protecting the Land of the Free,
Sergeant Major Peter Pacyao
Is now a mentor for JROTC.
As instructor at Baldwin High School,
He puts his experience to use
Training young students for the future:
Teaching discipline, not tolerating abuse.

Pacyao served our nation with pride—
The CSM of the 1st Brigade
Of the 1st Armored Division—
In Kosovo to the oppressed bringing aid.
He served in Herzegovina
And was involved in Desert Storm, too,
Going wherever he was needed,
Defending the Red, White, and Blue.

The students at Baldwin High School
Will treasure the training they receive
From Sergeant Major Pacyao—
Who shows them how in themselves to believe.
In the future, they will become leaders
Of our world and will look back with pride
At the JROTC program...
And at the mentor who is now at their side.

I shall conclude this visit to Baldwin High School with two photos taken in the classroom of CSM Peter E. Pacyao. The images speak for themselves....

Sergeant Major Peter E. Pacyao and Author Burgess in the JROTC Classroom at Baldwin High School

JROTC Class at Baldwin High School, February 2002

In 1994, another fine addition to the island of Maui opened its doors: The Maui Arts and Cultural Center. This center offers many events in the fields of art, music, and culture, as well as ongoing programs in music and dance. When I came to Maui in late August of 1995 to attend the Maui Writers' Conference for the first time, I saw an announcement about a special program being given at the Arts and Cultural Center. The program was entitled "Tales of Maui, the Demigod" and the program flyers indicated "an authentic Hawaiian performance. Meet Maui the Demigod through hula, chant, and storytelling". Needless to say, I attended the event. WOW! What an experience! I begin this visit to the Arts and Cultural Center with a photo of the site on which it is built....

As for the program on "Tales of Maui, the Demigod", it clearly showed me that...

Culture Is Alive on Maui

Maui is an island in the Hawaiian Island chain:
A land caressed by Tradewinds and by sweet "pineapple rain".
It's blessed with lots of sunshine and with starlit skies at night:
A Paradise for tourists—a vacationer's delight!

But Maui is much more than just an island in the sun.
It's rich in native culture that tells what has been done
As, through the eons, men and gods have played important roles
In molding Maui's history... and achieving valued goals.

The people on the island take pride in who they are
And dedicate their daily lives, not wishing on some star:
They're bringing to the world at large awareness of their past,
While fostering a sense of pride that's guaranteed to last!
The grownups teach their children the stories of their race
And make concerted efforts to bring them face to face
With folktales and mythology that make their culture live;
To make the past more meaningful for what it has to give
To future generations who, proud of their great race,
Will keep their heritage alive: their roots they will embrace!

The Maui Arts and Cultural Center opened in '94.
It's a tribute to Hawaiians and a great place to explore!
A highlight of a visit to Kahului town
Is a visit to this center: Be sure to come on down!

When I flew out to Maui in 1995,
I saw "The Tales of Maui" there, and Maui came alive!
The citizens of Maui did research on their land
And proudly showed an audience (which several times did stand)
Some stories of the life and times of Hawaii's Superman:
The demigod named Maui, who was both god and man.

The presentation made that night gave me the chance to see
The pride with which Hawaiians look back on history.
The stories of this demigod, for whom the isle is named,
Were brought to life with native chants, and all the scenes were framed
Within Hawaiian customs, explained in great detail
By fabulous narrations of each and ev'ry "tale".
The hula had a special role in almost ev'ry scene:
The movement in the dances told what the stories mean.

The audience that came to see this special Maui show
Both laughed and clapped at what they saw, for most of them did know
That what was taking place that night had filled them all with PRIDE:
A PRIDE they would gladly share, once they had come outside.

For me it was a special night, for I could feel the joy
That all those in the theatre—every girl and boy—
Experienced in watching as the past had come to life...
For now they all would take great pride in sharing Maui's life.

At the time of this visit to Maui, I had just begun serving on the Board of Directors of a local Repertory Theatre back in New Jersey. I became a member of the Maui Arts and Cultural Center and even purchased a set of bricks for the center's walkway: in memory of my parents and as a salute to my two friends from Wenatchee, Washington. I have attended many programs at the center, including an annual program presented by Keali'i Reichel on Valentine's Day Weekend. From 2001 to 2004, I planned my trip to Maui around his performance of music, dance, and culture.

I first heard the name of singer and entertainer Keali'i Reichel while attending the Maui Writers' Conference in 1995. This local resident was singing and playing guitar during breaks in the Conference sessions. Since 1995, Keali'i Reichel has become one of the most well-known singers on the islands, and his music has been recognized for its excellence on the Mainland.

What impresses me most about Keali'i is his focus on his Hawaiian background. He is always praising the youth of Hawaii and encouraging the young generation to keep alive the cultural heritage of a proud people. As for his musical talents, the best way to describe them is in a poetic salute to...

Keali'i Reichel

As you listen to the soft sounds of Tradewinds,
While sitting on an oceanfront lanai,
Gently caressing the palm fronds
That sway like hula dancers in the sky,
Listen carefully and you will encounter
The voice of a native Hawaiian
Singing sweetly about his culture
In songs with lyrics in Hawaiian.
This native sings with a special pride
In the heritage of which he is part:
He endeavors to carry on traditions
Of his race... and he sings from the heart!

This artist is the talented Keali'i Reichel
And his paintings, in songs and in chants,
Help keep alive the rhythmic beauty
Of the sounds that give US a chance
To understand why the palm fronds gently sway
As the Tradewinds blow serenely through the air...

Carrying melodies of a rich and honored culture;
Encouraging each of the listeners to share
In the wonderful "Spirit of Aloha"
That's extended to each keiki, wahine, and kane,
Bringing thoughts of love and kindness
Through the rhythm and charm of his mele.

Keali'i shares the story behind the song

In 2001, I arranged my stay on the island of Maui for the month of February so that I might be able to attend the annual Valentine's Day weekend performance of Keali'i Reichel at the Arts and Cultural Center. I was fortunate enough to get a seat in Row E (front row, seat 32: stage center!) I now come to Maui every February in order to attend his annual program.

Below is the ad that speaks of the 2001 program. On the next page, I begin my salute to the talents of Keali'i Reichel and to the many talented musicians, singers, and dancers who were part of that special evening....

Keali'i Reichel and his Grandmother

Kukahi 2001

Keali'i Reichel is a master:
He performs with his heart and his soul.
When enhanced by dancers and musicians,
His performance always reaches its goal.

More than two dozen hula dancers
Performed for the audience tonight:
Their hands in silent talk story;
Their smiles a visual delight.

A string sextet entertained us,
Along with a guitar quartet:
Background for the mele of Keali'i,
Along with a singing duet.

The lighting enhanced the dancing;
Keali'i enhanced the words;
The musicians enhanced the background;
The dancers enhanced what was heard.
The performance was thus a vessel
Seen floating on the spirit of the crowd,
Carrying those in attendance ever upward
Toward Heaven on a musical cloud.

Keali'i sang of his grandmother,
Whom he had known for thirty-eight years.
His life is a clear reflection
Of her joy, of her love, of her tears.
(In his youth, she guided him gently
With love, understanding, and support.
With her passing, her memory still remains,
Like a beacon guiding a ship to its port.)

Kukahi 2001 was, indeed,
A Ho'onananea delight:
A gift of Aloha from Hawaiians.

May we who received it tonight
Remember the words of Keali'i
As he sang of his "gramma" in praise:
"Don't forget to honor the ones whom we love
With our own 'Aloha', nights and days.
Don't wait until they've departed,
Then regret what we ought to have done.
Make the feeling of 'Aloha' perpetual...
It's that 'Aloha' that will make us all one."

Keali'i takes a quick peek at the audience

Kukahi 2003

The Maui Symphony Orchestra
Joined Keali'i Reichel
In his annual Valentine's Weekend Concert—
Every seat for three concerts did sell!
To produce a vibrant new depth in sound
For the mele Keali'i performed, *
While the Halau Ke'alaohamaile**
Described the mele in visual form.

The performers combined mele, new and old,
With a little talk story on the side...
And with solo, as well as group, hula,
Serving as the visual guide
Down a path of history and culture;
Of sadness, of hope, and of love.
The audience became part of the "ohana",***
Accompanied by sacred spirits from Above.

I went to the February 15 concert
And, as always, sat in the front row,
In my favorite seat, E-26,
To enjoy Keali'i's great show.

*"Mele" is Hawaiian for "song"
**"Halau" is Hawaiian for "school"
***"Ohana" is Hawaiian for "family"

Prior to each of the performances of Keali'i Reichel at the Arts and Cultural Center, attendees have a chance to observe the work of some of the talented artisans on the islands and to learn about the stories behind the works of art on display. In February 2002, I spoke with Ku'ulei Martinson, a quilt maker who had on display one of the handwoven kiheipeli (memory blankets). One side contained images of important historical and cultural sites in Hawaii; the reverse had images of the plants and flowers associated with the islands.

When I returned to Maui for the 2003 Kukahi concert, we met again—and she still had this magnificent kiheipeli, in king size. I purchased it and she personally signed one of the images for me. It now rests proudly on my bed and continues to inspire dreams of future visits to the islands—and conversations with other talented artisans. Ku'ulei gave me permission to include a photo of the kiheipeli and a photo of her signing the one image for me. The third photo shows Ku'ulei and her husband Martin. (Note: Martin was born on the Big Island and participates in the annual Royal Court Procession at the heiau on "The Hill of the Whale" in Kawaihae in August. It is he who invited me to attend the 2003 event and cultural festival!)

I am a volunteer in a number of nursing homes and assisted living complexes in New Jersey. When I travel, I take my camcorder to bring back some video memories to share with the residents. I have an 8mm camcorder and, as a result, need to transfer the videos onto VHS in order to show them. On one of my visits to Maui, I discovered a store called Hawaii Video Memories and found out that the employees do the transfers, at a very reasonable price. I bring my 8mm videos in on the first day of each visit and drop them off with employee Nichol Nagata. Then, before I leave the island, I return and pick up the copies. When I stopped in on February 13, 2001, what I found was the inspiration for a poem on...

A Magical Maui Moment

Magical moments on Maui
Occur to visitors and to residents as well...
In Kihei, Paia, and Lahaina:
Moments one can't always foretell.

On a recent visit to the island,
In February 2001,
Came a moment that I'll always cherish
Long after my traveling is done.
I had come to a store in Kahului
That helps keep one's memories alive:
To Hawaii Video Memories.
What a moment as I did arrive!
I had taken two 8mm videos
To be duplicated onto VHS
And had returned to pick up the copies.
What occurred was magical, nothing less.

Nichol Nagata greeted me,
Along with a bundle of joy:
A fifty-day-old Maui resident,
Joshua, her new baby boy.

The photo I took that morning,
Of Nichol and her precious new son,
Provided a magical memory for me,
Of joy 'neath the bright Maui sun.

213

Nichol Nagata and seven-week-old Joshua

As Tony Van Steen says: "You never know what life has in store." In December of 2001, I received a special holiday greeting card, from Nichol and her co-workers Marc, Todd, Scott, Tom, and Bob—six of Santa's helpers on the island of Maui.

I was truly honored and excited when an invitation arrived from Nichol and her husband Kyle: an invitation to come to Joshua's first birthday party. I later learned that the first birthday of a child in Hawaii is a special event, a fact that made me even more proud to think that I would be invited to be part of the occasion.

I made special arrangements to fly to Maui for the January 19, 2002, celebration for Joshua Philip Nagata. Attendance at the party inspired a poem, describing...

Joshua Philip Nagata's 1st Birthday:

A Special Occasion

A special celebration for youth in Hawaii
Takes place one year after birth,
With family and friends all gathered around
Proclaiming the first year on Earth
Of a new Hawaiian citizen...
It's a day of traditional joy.

On Saturday, the nineteenth of January,
The focus was on a young boy:
One-year-old Joshua Nagata
Was the young guest of honor that day.
Surrounded by many close relatives,
Joshua did smile, crawl, and play.

His parents, Nichol and Kyle,
Were congratulated by every guest.
The first member of the next generation
Of Nagatas soon would begin his great quest
For success and good health on the islands...
He's already achieved his first goal:
One full year of exciting adventures;
Of learning; of enriching his soul.

The theme for his party was "Winnie the Pooh"
And the keiki table had quite a display:
Pictures for the children to color
With crayons—there even was gray (!);
Pooh hats and a special lollipop treat;
Birthday balloons on each chair;
A special "Pooh crayon / pen holder";

216

Pooh images could be seen everywhere!
The meal, buffet-style, was "ono"
And included raw fish, rice, and poi:
'Twas a typical luau-style banquet
That had every guest smiling with joy.
Following the meal came a juggler
Who was a balloon man as well.
He made kittens, dogs, balloon swords, and airplanes:
Balloon toys that really were swell.

The video highlight of the party
Was a still-photo, live-action show:
A summary of Joshua's first fun-filled year...
Sleeping, eating, on the go.

Then came the anticipated moment
When Joshua was presented his cake.
While everyone sang "Happy Birthday",
What a great move he did make...
While Mom helped him blow out the candle,
He reached out his right arm with glee,
Grabbed a fistful of cake and then, smiling,
(Just like POOH with some honey, you see)
Began eating and licking his fingers...
He'd been waiting so long for this treat.
His family and friends just applauded,
While Joshua continued to eat.

Special greetings were extended to everyone
By Joshua's proud mom and dad,
As well as by Joshua's Uncle Daniel.
He was nervous, but also quite glad,
To see so many close friends and relatives
In attendance at Joshua's big day.
Daniel knew these first birthday memories
Would never from their minds fade away.

Nichol Nagata and son Joshua: January 19, 2002

My expression of congratulations and of thanks in poetry to the Nagata family has resulted in my becoming a member of the "ohana" and in my having opportunities that are extended to very few visitors from the mainland. In December of 2002, Joshua sent me a Christmas greeting, shown on this page.

Thanks, Nichol, Kyle, and Joshua. Your friendship is appreciated.

An excellent tour company on the island of Maui is Ekahi Tours. The local drivers offer the visitor some unequaled experiences in history and culture. I traveled to Hana, experienced a Haleakala sunrise, learned about the growing and cultivating of taro and other native plants, and saw firsthand the pride of local Hawaiians on my tours with Ekahi. These experiences led me to set up a special Ekahi tour for my teaching colleagues in 1998. A truly unique experience was that of witnessing the preparation of food for a luau in a local imu: a luau feast at the reception following the wedding of the Ekahi Tours' owner's son.

Nothing could summarize this experience like a series of photographs....

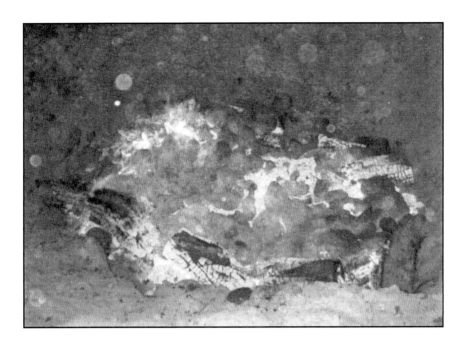

Preparing of the imu for the wedding reception luau

After twelve hours, the imu is opened and the food is removed and pre-pared for the luau

In the late 1990s, a new Borders Books & Music store opened in the Maui Marketplace in Kahului. On a regular basis, Borders provided opportunities for local performers to entertain patrons. One afternoon, the musical guests were to be one of the most well-known slack-key guitar players on the islands, his wife, who performed hula, and his mother, who sang, talked story, and chanted about the natural beauty of the islands. I requested permission to photograph the family, the Beamers. When I returned home, I sent copies of the photos to them, along with a poem that was inspired by their performance....

A Tribute to the Beamers

Each culture has a special way
To celebrate her past:
Through music, dance, and arts and crafts
Her people's lifestyles last.
The talents of the residents
Help us to understand
The ways of life in many worlds:
Their legacy is grand!

The Beamers are Hawaiians
Who share their way of life
In a way that only locals can:
They celebrate that life!
They share by "talking story"
And as each tale is told,
It's presented with music and with dance
As the storyline unfolds.
The matriarch of the family—
Nona is her name—
Presents the tales of ancient times.
Each tale ignites a flame
Inside the soul of everyone
Who listens as present does she
A wondrous collection of stories:
The Golden Lehua Tree.
Nona's son, Keola Beamer,
Accompanies her on guitar,
While Keola's wife performs each tale
In dance, known near and far.
The swaying hips and moving hands
Echo Nona's voice
As the movements of the hula
Allow us to rejoice.

The Beamers in a performance at Borders Books & Music in Kahului: February 2000

Nona Beamer autographs copies of *The Golden Lehua Tree* CD while Keola talks with fans following the performance at Borders

My next destinations are Paia and Kuau. When you ask local residents of Maui about these two towns, a common response is that...

Paia and Kuau
Are the windsurfers' domain.
They come to ride
From far and wide:
It's here they love to train.

Both of these towns are located on the road that leads to Hana, the town most well-known for being the final resting place of aviator Charles A. Lindbergh. As you drive through Paia, if you turn right at the only traffic light in town, the road will take you past an old sugar mill and then on to the Doris Todd Memorial Christian School. How did I know the location of this school? While on a whale watch excursion in December of 1998, I met two instructors from the school. They were on board gathering information for their classes. When they discovered that I was an educator and a poet, they invited me to attend the Annual Christmas program at Doris Todd. Two days later, I came to the school, met with the principal, attended the program, and was inspired to compose a poem about the presentation, entitled "What in the World Is Christmas?" I chose to use a Hawaiian expression for the title of the selection, and that title seems fitting to the overall theme of this book. I thank the students of the school for giving me the inspiration for...

Aloha Ke Akua
(God Is Love)

I had gone to the island of Maui:
I'd be spending the holidays there.
While staying near the town of Paia,
I visited an elementary school there.
Students at the Doris Todd Memorial Christian School
Were presenting their annual show:
"What in the World Is Christmas?"
I decided to that program I'd go.

The students wore national clothing
From countries all over the world.
They explained how the season of Christmas
Is celebrated by both young and old:
The ringing of bells, the posadas,
Gifts that are left 'neath the tree—
All representing traditions
That fill all our spirits with glee.

As the students sang various carols,
Describing this Season of Joy,
They sang about the meaning of Christmas,
The day that brings everyone joy:
The day of the birth of Christ Jesus,
Whose LOVE saves us all from our sin.
The students, from many world cultures,
Joined hands, asking the audience to join in...
"For it's time that we all come together
To learn of our true Savior's LOVE",
Understanding that "Aloha Ke Akua",
As the Lord sends HIS Grace from Above.

What a beautiful holiday program!
I'm so happy that I had been there,
For the faces of all those young students
Reflected the LOVE they will share
As into the twenty-first century
They carry God's LOVE far and near,
Working together in friendship,
Sharing that LOVE without fear.

The then principal of the school, Carolyn Moore, shared with me an article that appeared in the February 26, 1996, issue of *The Maui News*. I thought that you, the reader of this collection of poems and photos, would enjoy reading some excerpts from the article, entitled "A Labor of Love, Faith, and Commitment". The article was written by *Maui News* staff writer Claudine San Nicolas.

The Reverend Edward Todd, now 83 years old, returned to Maui last week to celebrate the 40th anniversary of the school that bears his late wife's name.

"It's the Doris Todd Memorial Christian School," he said. "The word 'Christian' is sometimes dropped off, but it's very important."

Doris Todd Memorial Christian School came about because of the Todd's love for the Lord and a commitment to share their faith with children. The school's lofty mission is to "provide a Christ-centered, biblically directed education which instills the desire and practice of academic excellence, moral integrity, patriotism and church involvement to the glory of God."

It all began on Maui in April 1954, when the Todds initiated the Hawaiian Islands mission after serving six years in the Philippines. Two years later, they opened a preschool in a plantation home in Haiku. After the first year, word about the preschool got around Paia and, before they knew it, the Todds had 13 children signed up. They moved out of the house and ran the school from a building in Paia town. Eventually that building also got too small and they moved again, to the Paia Youth Center.

Todd recalled the 1960 tidal wave that destroyed homes and took out a large pavilion at Baldwin Beach Park. The school building was the only structure left standing on the ocean side. "We believe the Lord had everything to do with it," Todd said. 'I think He was showing us He wanted us to continue."

The next year, the Todds successfully negotiated for and took over the property upon which the present campus sits on Baldwin Avenue. In 1962, Paia Baptist School, as it was called, added a 1st Grade class. The school was renamed Doris Todd Memorial Christian School after Mrs. Todd died in June, 1965.

Principal Moore said the school is negotiating for more land and hopes to build more classrooms.

I stopped by the school during my September 2002 visit and was greeted by a sign that would indicate that negotiations have been successful and that the school will be growing in the future.

Since my first visit to the school in December 1998, I have returned to visit again on four occasions. On one visit, I wore my special patriotic outfit—a gift from the students of the Project Memorial Foundation Committee at Audubon High School in Audubon, New Jersey, in thanks for my patriotic efforts on their behalf. As I was walking from one class to another across the campus, I found myself surrounded by a group of young students at the school who, seeing me dressed from head to toe in red, white, and blue, began serenading me by singing "The Star-Spangled Banner". WOW! What a memorable moment. (I was both pleased AND amazed by this gesture of friendship and patriotism. However, it is evident that one of the missions of the Doris Todd Memorial Christian School has been accomplished!)

The following photos are included in this collection as a thank-you to the students and to the faculty of the school for some cherished memories of my visits to their campus in Paia.

I come back down Baldwin Avenue to the traffic light and turn right. At a distance of some three miles from Downtown Paia sets one of the most scenic locations on all of the islands: Mama's Fish House, a seafood restaurant nestled in a little cove with its own beachfront and with an ambiance that is completely Hawaiian.

> Each time I travel to Maui
> For a one-week vacation (or two),
> New people I meet
> And great seafood I eat:
> There's always so much I can do.
> Mama's Fish House is first on my checklist:
> I eat there at least three or four times.
> The service is great
> And the entrees first rate…
> Plus the setting inspires my rhymes!

At the recommendation of some friends, my mother and I went for lunch at Mama's during a stay in 1991. We both enjoyed the experience so much that we returned to the restaurant the following summer. The greeting that awaited us was unexpected: The manager of the restaurant, seeing us come in, took us to the same table we had had the year before. Martin Lenny remembered us and said he thought we would enjoy sitting at the same table. What a memory! And what an impression that show of "Aloha" made! I was so grateful that I first wrote a poem and then continued to dine at Mama's on every visit to Maui, even staying in one of the beachfront cottages on one occasion.

When I began to work on this book, I approached Mr. Floyd Christienson, the owner of the restaurant, and asked permission to use photos taken at Mama's on the covers of this collection. As you can see, he granted permission.

Here are a few more examples of the breathtaking beauty to be seen at Kuau Cove….

Entrance to Mama's

As you can see, Mama's Fish House is the perfect spot on the island to come for some…

Beachfront Dining

What a setting for a great seafood dinner,
Near Paia on Route 36,
Nestled snugly in tropical beauty:
One of Maui's top restaurant picks.
The name of the spot: Mama's Fish House
And inside, the motif is unique:
The decor is completely Hawaiian,
With some idols of jade and of teak.
On the walls are artistic reminders
Of the culture to which you're exposed…
From the beauty of picturesque artwork
To shell necklaces on beams stately posed.
During dinner you're treated to music
That is strictly Hawaiian in style,
And the cuisine is quite varied and "ono"…
Making choices may take you a while.
There are ten ways to order an entree,
Maybe grilled, perhaps baked, or sautéed,
And the freshness of all of the seafood
Makes the meal worth the price that is paid.
From the wine list and choice of great cocktails
To the loaf of just-baked, homemade bread;
From delicious fish chowder or salad
To some cake (or some ice cream, instead);
Every course is prepared to perfection
And the service is "A NUMBER 1"…
With a staff that knows just what is needed
From the moment it greets everyone.
There's much more I could say about Mama's,
It is truly a dining delight.
But you'll never find out 'til you've been there…
How 'bout going for dinner tonight!

Martin Lenny and one of the hostesses greet visitors to Mama's

Dennis Daly and one of the receptionists take reservations for lunch

Mama's adds some holiday color to the Hawaiian décor with some poinsettias

How about coming to Mama's for dinner?

I did invite you to dinner at Mama's—so let's go! I am bringing along a friend of mine from Maui, Diana Stuart. I first met Diana at a poetry convention in Washington, D.C., in the early nineties. I couldn't believe it when she told me that she lives in Kihei! (That is where I have my timeshare units!)

In the Hawaiian tradition, torches are lighted just as the sun is setting. I captured Assistant Manager Kevin O'Malley doing the honors the evening that Diana and I went for dinner....

Kevin O'Malley lights torches on the beach at Mama's

The following morning, I spoke with Diana by phone and then composed this selection about...

An Evening at Mama's Fish House

"Diana, did you enjoy your dinner
At Mama's Fish House last night?
Please tell my readers about it
And describe the picturesque site."
"What an incredible dinner I had
At Mama's Fish House last night!
Craig told me I would enjoy it:
It indeed was a dining delight!
From our table, which looked out on the beachfront,
We were witness to Nature's display
As the sun slowly set in the distance
And the Tradewinds with the palm trees did play.
As the music played softly around us,
We were served a fabulous meal:
Homemade bread, appetizer, and entrée,
All of which have a great taste appeal!
The service is truly outstanding
And the setting indeed is unique…
When YOU come to Maui, come to Mama's!
For fine food it has all you may seek."

"Thanks, Diana, I'm glad you enjoyed it.
Thanks also to Mama's great 'crew':
The staff knows how to make beachfront dining
An experience that will not make you blue!"

After dining, I took a walk around the restaurant to capture some of the beauty of
Mama's at night. One of those photos proved both patriotic and mysterious….

I have been fortunate in being able to spend the Christmas holidays in Hawaii on three different occasions. While on Maui, I even found one home that had a Christmas greeting spelled out in lights on the roof: "Mele Kalikimaka" (Merry Christmas). One morning I decided to go to Azeka Place for breakfast and found that fir trees were on sale. When I approached the area to investigate, I saw Santa Claus and learned about how he receives help from local "residents" when delivering gifts to the children. I was very happy to know that…

Santa Comes to Maui

I was born in the state of New Jersey
And have lived there all of my life
In the same house in the town of Audubon:
Never have I taken a wife.
I'm familiar with the Christmas tradition:
Leaving cookies and milk by the tree
So that Santa (when his sleigh and eight reindeer
Land on the rooftops with glee)
Will discover my own special present
In thanks for the gifts he will leave,
Left with the love which all children
Share on each Christmas Eve.

But the reindeer are used to cold weather:
Their warm coats and sure hooves serve them well
As they carry the world's Christmas treasures.
They love this annual job, you can tell.

On a recent vacation to Maui
I learned that the reindeer get help
From the dolphin and fish of the islands
That, after a special meal of kelp,
Gather together in Kihei
And are harnessed to a strongly built surfboard
That will carry gifts over the seas
And onto the palm trees and beachfronts
For delivery to the children with ease.

I spoke with St. Nick down in Kihei
As he collected some lists from the kids.
He explained how the bottlenose dolphin
Had rescued his sleigh from the sea
When the heat of the tropical climate
Caused the reindeer to faint and fall free...
The dolphin, along with some ahi,
Decided to help Santa's cause:
They carried the gifts through the Tropics—
Their scales thus replacing the paws.

On radar, there is no distinction
Between dolphin and tiny reindeer:
By working together, both creatures
Help Santa make his rounds every year.

The residents of the islands are happy
That the dolphin and ahi help out,
And many displays for the season
Leave in one's mind little doubt
That Santa is helped in his mission—
Bringing joy to all Christmas Eve—
By these creatures well known on the islands:
Much praise and respect they receive!

As the lines of the poem indicate, Santa exchanges his sleigh for a surfboard
and, at times, an outrigger canoe, while the reindeer are replaced by "reinfish".
Every year at Chuck's Steak House, in Kihei Town Center, the owners put up
a display, showing Santa in action on a surfboard. At Mama's Fish House, a
display at the entrance to the restaurant shows Santa in his canoe, being pulled
by reinfish. In the lead is the famous character from the islands, Rudolph the
Red-Nosed Reinfish.

Taking Diana Stuart to dinner was my way of thanking her for all she has shown me on Maui over the past decade. I can best summarize that friendship in verse.

Diana Stuart

As an educator, historian, and poet
I have made Maui my second home.
When I come, I stay in the Kihei area:
From there, o'er the island I roam.
I attend an annual poetry event,
Sponsored by I.S.P.:
It's held in our nation's capitol,
In Washington, D.C.
While conversing with some poetic friends
Who come to this event each year,
I was talking of my love for Maui
When one of the participants drew near:
"Did you say you travel to Maui?
May I ask in which area you stay?"
"I always stay in Kihei Town."
I was amazed when I heard her say:
"My name is Diana Stuart.
I live in Kihei Town.
The next time you visit the island,
Call me and I'll show you around."
Diana volunteers as an usher
At the Arts and Cultural Center.
In addition she works, on a part-time basis,
At an Island Activities Center.
Each time I travel to Maui,
Diana shows me something new:
From one of her favorite restaurants
To a lookout with a scenic view.
She invited me to the Old Lahaina Luau;
Showed me the Diamond Resort;
Took me to the Scenic SeaWatch Restaurant;
Talked about the island's seaport.

Mahalo nui loa, Diana,
Your friendship is special to me.
I can't wait for my next trip to Maui...
And what you've arranged for me to see.

Diana Stuart joins in the festivities of the Boar's Head Feast on December 16, 1995

Diana Stuart and Author Burgess at a luau in 1996

Less than half a mile from Mama's on Route 36, heading for the Hana Highway, is Hookipa, the famous windsurfing beach at Kuau. From the parking lot at Mama's, you can see dozens of windsurfers taking advantage of the currents and the Tradewinds. Two photos say it all....

From Kuau, the road leads to Hana. The trip may take three hours to complete and can be a driving challenge. Yet it is a worthwhile excursion because the natural beauty is spectacular, with views of high cliffs, waterfalls, and lookout sites that will take your breath away. As is often said...

The scenic road to Hana
Offers views beyond compare.
It's quite a drive,
But you'll survive...
Take the challenge, if you dare!

When the visitor arrives, he or she will find a small church and, on its property, the gravesite of aviator Charles Lindbergh. It is easy to understand why Lindbergh chose Hana as his home on Maui. The following photos of the trip I took to Hana will give you an idea of the beauty of the landscape along the eastern side of the island....

One of the beautiful waterfalls on the road to Hana

On the road to Hana, overlooking one of the fifty-four one-lane bridges

The gravesite of Charles Lindbergh in Hana. The building barely seen in the background is a church.

Waianapanapa Caves
and Black Sand Beach near Hana

The caves are actually lava tubes
Created by eruptions in the past;
The beach is surrounded by lava rocks,
Sentinels that for ages will last;
The black sand evolved over centuries
From interaction with the waters of the sea.

Waianapanapa is stunning,
Filled with images for the memory.

The beach is accessible by walking
Along a pathway, both scenic and pristine.
The visitor can enter the lava tubes
With caution—lava rock cuts can be mean.

Standing on the beach, near the water,
One natural image is observed:
A lava rock bridge near the shoreline,
A creation of Madame Pele now preserved
For visitors who come to Waianapanapa
During a tour to Hana, Maui, and beyond.

Come early and wander in silence...
Of this site you will soon become fond.

A view of the Lava Rock Bridge with the caves to the right of the beach area

On the return trip from Hana, the visitor finds him or herself back in the town of Kahului. From there, another exciting adventure can begin: a trip to the Upcountry region of the island and a drive up to the summit of Haleakala. As the trip begins, be sure to stop at the town of Makawao: a town that looks like a photo from the days of the Wild West on the Mainland. It is a quaint town and one filled with history and culture. Every Fourth of July, a parade is held in Makawao. In the mid-1990s, I drove up to Makawao to see this parade. It was a wonderful experience, and I had opportunities to speak with some local residents who told me much about "the early days" in this area. I even received some hints on how to identify horses and how to understand a little bit about their personality.

Fourth of July Parade in Makawao

On July 5 of that year, I drove to the Upcountry region again, visiting an incredible flower nursery in Kula, the Tedeschi Winery, where I had the chance to taste pineapple wine, and the Thompson Ranch, where I experienced my FIRST EVER horseback ride. The information I received from the locals at the parade in Makawao proved helpful—and what a ride it was, riding on the slopes of Haleakala at sunset! The horse I rode was carefully selected for a "beginner", and we had a great conversation with statements like: "Nice horse" and "Be gentle. Remember, this is my first ride." We actually got along quite well, especially considering that I kept trying to use my camcorder to get some shots of the sunset—while remaining in the saddle!

The road to the Upcountry region then can take the visitor to the 10,002-foot summit of the Haleakala volcano....

> Oh, yes, there is a volcano
> Named Haleakala.
> The color tones
> Of the crater cones
> Will make you "Ooh" and "Aah".
> You must go there for the sunrise:
> It will take your breath away!
> When you depart,
> Within your heart
> The majestic scenes will stay.

The photo on this page was taken just after dawn, on February 8, 2001, as the sun's rays touched one of the silversword plants: a plant that can be found only near the summit of Haleakala. After thirty years of growing, the silversword plant blooms just once and then dies....

The following poem was written after my third visit to Haleakala for the sunrise. I had gone with Ekahi Tours on February 8, 2001, and was once again anticipating the beauty of...

Haleakala at Sunrise

It begins with an early wakeup call—
At three-thirty A.M. or so—
And a two-hour ride to the summit
To greet cloud banks passing below.

The wind chill may be in the twenties
As you await a breathtaking view:
Haleakala at sunrise,
With colors of every hue
Reflecting off the cinder cones
In the volcanic crater world:
Colors that change by the moment
As Haleakala's beauty is unfurled.

The sunlight continues to strengthen,
Revealing a remarkable sight:
The leaves of the precious silversword plant,
Glistening in the dawn's early light.

Should you take this journey—as I did—
On the morning of a brilliant full moon,
The sunrise and moonset images
Will be etched in your memory and, soon,
Will call you back to the summit
To observe this breathtaking view
Of sunrise, of moonset, of silversword life:
A return journey you just can't refuse!

Visitors are reminded about the change in temperature that will be experienced on this trip to the summit. At 4:45 A.M., the temperature may be in the low thirties (F) and, if conditions are right, the wind chill may dip into the teens and a snow flurry may be seen. So it was on my first sunrise adventure. Two of the visitors in my van chose NOT to believe the reminders and wore only bathing suits to the summit that morning. (After all, in Kihei, it was already in the sixties by 3:30 A.M.) Needless to say, they regretted THAT decision.

Many visitors take on a unique challenge when they come to the summit to observe the sunrise. They then bicycle thirty-seven miles down from the summit into Paia. And now some photos to capture your imagination....

The splendor of the cinder cones in the crater of Haleakala

Bicyclists prepare for the thirty-seven-mile trip from the summit of Haleakala to the town of Paia

The shadow of the author just after dawn at the summit of Haleakala

On one occasion, I drove to the summit in the late afternoon to experience the sunset. The summit world was nothing like it is in the early morning. The colors are dazzling, and the views of Maui and of the neighboring islands are unforgettable.

On the road to the summit, the visitor will pass a number of ranches, with both horses and cattle. The afternoon I drove to the summit, I was surprised on my return to find a cow standing in the middle of the road. It took some diplomacy, but the cow decided to move to the side in order that I might get by—a nice gesture of the "Spirit of Aloha" on her part.

A cattle ranch on the road to the summit of Haleakala

View from the 10,002-foot summit of Haleakala

Sunset from Haleakala

A unique experience for me was my first encounter with the process of harvesting the sugarcane in the fields. As the cane is prepared for harvesting, the fields in which the cane is growing are first set on fire... resulting in what I call...

Sugarcane Rain

I awakened quite early one morning,
And was startled by what I did see:
Black cinders had covered my unit's lanai!
Now, what in the world could it be?

When I opened the door to the lanai,
I could smell something strange in the air.
And, since I don't live in Hawaii,
I could with it not one thing compare.
As the breeze began blowing more strongly,
A strange cloud slowly passed overhead:
It was dense and like caramel in color,
Yet its "moisture" was blacker than lead!
When I tried to examine the cinders,
They disintegrated right in my hand...
Yet the grass and the lanai were covered
With a coating of this dusty black "sand"!

It was then that I finally realized
What was hap'ning around me that morn:
They were burning a section of the cane field:
That's where those black cinders were born!
For the sugarcane harvest in Maui
Begins with the fields set ablaze,
But for the tourists who don't know what's hap'ning,
The resulting black rain will amaze...

For they've all heard of showers on Maui,
But they are known as sweet "pineapple rain".
How amazing to see those BLACK showers...
Which I now know is burnt sugarcane.

262

The burning of the sugarcane in a field near Pu'unene on September 6, 1995

Cane field waiting to be harvested, following the burning stage

Over the years, I have spoken with many local residents about the process involved in the production of sugar from the sugarcane. I learned from these locals that one of the negative side-effects of the ongoing burning of the cane fields is the increase in cases of asthma and of other respiratory problems in the young residents. I was reminded of these comments while waiting for a flight one morning at Kahului Airport, for I was an eyewitness to a...

Sugarcane Sunrise

The petals of dawn had prepared us
For the blossoming of the sun,
Its bright yellow bloom in splendor
Announcing that nighttime was done.

How surprising to see the bloom fading
As it rose through an ominous cloud,
Exploding skyward from the fields of sugarcane,
Engulfing the sun in a shroud.

That bloom, once golden in color...
Was transformed by the fiery cane
Into shades of orange and caramel:
A cloud from the violent terrain.

To the novice it resembled a tornado
Being guided by an unforgiving eye
That stared from its blood-soaked socket,
Ascending into the early morning sky.

This poem was inspired by what I observed on the morning of Wednesday, September 13, 2000, at 6:55 A.M. I did not get the photo developed until several weeks later and was amazed at how well it reflected the image described in the poem....

A view of the sun rising behind the smoke produced by the burning of a cane field near Kahului Airport

The last part of our visit to Maui will take us from Kahului into the areas of Kihei, Wailea, and Makena....

Kihei offers beaches
With miles of fine white sand:
The ideal spot
To bring your tot.
It's a great place to get tanned!

Wailea and Makena
Have tennis courts galore;
Golf courses grand
With their traps of sand;
Hiking trails to explore.

Within the past decade, these three areas have seen much growth, with new shopping malls, resort destinations, and residential housing. The visitor can avoid some of the local traffic in the Kihei area by turning onto Route 31, which will take him or her directly to the resorts, tennis courts, and golf courses in Wailea. The tourist will miss out, however, by not coming along the South Kihei Road area. The first site encountered along South Kihei Road is the Kihei Canoe Club. This club is the topic of my first poem for this part of Maui....

The Kihei Canoe Club

When first I came to the Kihei Canoe Club,
The colors of the canoes greeted me:
Bright reds and yellows called "Aloha"
From the outriggers that sat by the sea.
I parked my car and walked over
To what, for me, was a wonderful sight:
Six outrigger canoes lined up gracefully,
Gleaming in the Kihei sunlight.
I took sev'ral photos of these vessels
While wondering about where they'd been...
And dreaming about the adventures
They had had in the races they'd been in.

The canoes brought to mind the last segment
Of each episode of *Hawaii Five-0:*
The team members rowing in unison
As the canoes through the waters would go.

Two years later, I came back to the Canoe Club
To watch as a dream would come true:
I would talk with a coach and team members,
Then observe what each rower would do...
The young Hawaiians had gathered
On the beach at the Canoe Club again
To prepare for a canoe competition:
They received their assignments and then
Carried their canoes through the breakers,
Got on board and paddled as one...
Overcoming the currents and crosswinds
In the glow of the afternoon sun.

Canoes line the beach at the Kihei Canoe Club following an early morning practice

Team members carry their canoe into the water for a practice run on February 9, 2001

Ready to compete

Coach Brady gives encouragement to the team members

Three times each week the teams practice
To prepare for the next weekend's race.
With each practice, the members rowed better
As each team learned to "pick up the pace".

Coach Robert Brady kept active
As the outriggers "picked up the pace".
He shouted encouragement to each captain,
The same as he would in a race.
When the rowers completed the first lap,
Coach Brady gave advice to each crew,
While running through the waves near the shoreline:
Then each team rowed away on lap two.

The practice session now over,
The canoes were brought back on the beach:
The youth and the coach were ready
And would for the next goal now reach.

As for me, what a thrilling experience,
Observing the youth rowing with ease:
Challenging each other to row better
As the outriggers cut a course through the seas.

After a successful practice session, members bring the canoes back onto the beach at the Kihei Canoe Club

Of the many experiences I have had while visiting the islands, one stands out in my mind as reflecting the history and culture of the Hawaiian people. The experience resulted from a conversation I had with the coach of the Kihei Canoe Club. When I explained to him that I was interested in learning more about the club and of its activities and events, he told me about a special event that was to take place on the Kihei beach on Sunday, February 11, 2001. I came to the event and witnessed the majesty of...

Hōkule'a Maui 2001

Each time that I come to Hawaii,
New experiences are waiting for me:
Each island provides opportunities
To learn more about history,
As well as to meet local residents
Willing to share what they know
With visitors who take time to listen...
That's one way in which friendships grow.

On one of my visits to Maui,
I saw young Hawaiians in teams
At the picturesque Kihei Canoe Club.
(Is rowing as hard as it seems?)
I took time to watch as they practiced
In awe of their strength and their skill;
I took some fascinating photographs
As each team took part in a drill.

When I told the coach of my interest
In learning more about what I'd seen,
He informed me about Hōkule'a:
What it is; where it's been; what it means.
This brief afternoon conversation
Was the beginning of a voyage unique,
For I learned much about sailing history
And into Polynesian culture did peek.

Hōkūle'a is the name of Hawaii's Zenith Star
That passes directly overhead each night...
And may have been a guide for navigators
On voyages that depended on sight.

A replica of an ancient voyaging canoe
Was built with a purposeful aim:
To prove that a vessel, traditional in style,
Could verify what oral histories claim.

The Hōkūle'a, launched on March the eighth
In nineteen seventy-five,
Began a twenty-five-year voyage of discovery...
Bringing Polynesian culture alive.
Guided by seabirds, the sun, stars, and winds,
And the swells on the tempestuous seas,
The Hōkūle'a, a sixty-two-foot-long voyaging canoe,
Brought to life those oral histories:
Sailing through South Pacific waters;
Rediscovering voyages of the past;
Reawakening pride in a culture
That long into the future will last.

I was there at the Kihei Canoe Club
In the calendar year 2001:
On Sunday, the eleventh of February,
In the brilliance of the noonday sun.
I witnessed a special ceremony
At the "canoe pohaku ahu",
A special shrine to voyagers:
A ceremony conducted by a "kumu".

The event, spiritual in nature,
On Ka Lae Pohaku Beach,
Brought together the youth and the elders:
Far beyond that site did it reach.

Hōkūle'a Maui 2001
Is an experience I'll never forget,

For I watched as the youth on the island
Honored modern-day sailors whom they'd met:
Sailors who took on the challenge
Of navigating without computerized aids;
Retracing ancestral voyages,
Guided by the stars and the "Trades".

The ceremony on the beach in Kihei
Reflected a time-honored past,
When traditions meant more than present-day fads
That vanish—with no reason to last.

The experience provided me reason to praise
The efforts of residents of the isle:
Residents who help keep history alive,
Using examples in traditional style.

Following the ceremony, I spoke with several of the elders in attendance. I then followed the Hōkūle'a over to Maalaea Harbor and had a chance to speak with several members of her crew and a number of the young people who had come to meet with the crewmembers. What you will see now is a photo summary of the experience....

HŌKŪLE'A
MĀLAMA HAWAI'I

NĀ WAIWAI
Guiding Values

★★★★

Aloha
To love

Mālama
To care for

'Imi 'Ike
To seek knowledge

Lokomaika'i
To share with each other

Na'au Pono
To nurture a deep sense of justice

Ola kino Maika'i
To live healthily

★★★★

POLYNESIAN VOYAGING SOCIETY
HAWAI'I MARITME CENTER

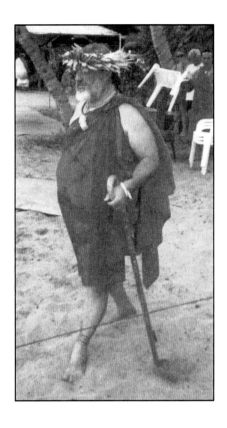

Preparations for the ceremony are now complete

Members of the Kihei Canoe Club welcome the crew of Hōkūle'a in traditional Dance and Chant on Sunday, February 11, 2001

Members of royalty on the island talk about the importance of the ceremony

Participants proceed to the Stone Temple for the ceremony during which a new stone will be added to the temple

The new stone waits to join those from canoe clubs around the world following the ceremony on February 11, 2001

The Hōkūle'a Stone joins the "ohana" following the traditional waiting period (center right)

Visitors come aboard the Hōkūle'a at Maalaea Harbor following the welcoming ceremony in Kihei

Directly across the street from the Kihei Canoe Club is Suda's Market. Outside the market, one of the island's master carvers has his workshop. Tevitas invites visitors to observe him as he creates his wood carvings and, should a visitor decide to make a purchase, he will carve a special inscription on the base for him or her.

During one of my visits, I asked permission to take some photographs of Tevitas "at work", and he allowed me to include several of them in this "Fleeting Glimpse of Paradise".

Master Carver Tevitas begins work on detailing of a new item in his "studio" on South Kihei Road

Work begins on a new carving

The HaleAloha Studio of Tevitas, next to the Suda Market on Kihei Road, in September 2003

The works of Master Carver Tevitas

Visitors admire the quality of the carvings prior to making a purchase

The islands of Hawaii have produced some outstanding talent in the field of music: musicians and vocalists who entertain local residents and visitors with a unique desire to share their talent and their cultural knowledge of the islands.

On one of my first visits to Maui, I saw an announcement about a performance of Hawaiian music at the Maui Lu Resort in Kihei: a performance given by Mr. Jesse Nakooka, a gentleman with the nickname "Mr. Maui". What a fascinating show—a combination of piano playing, singing, and talk story. Mr. Nakooka related childhood memories, combined with special songs—including one about the hat he was wearing and one about the "fifty-four bridges to Hana". I had a chance to speak with "Mr. Maui" after the show, and from that time on, I always looked for information about his shows. In recent years, he has stopped performing, but I shall never forget the memories that came from listening to "Mr. Maui".

Jesse Nakooka

I was talking with Jesse Nakooka
In the Maui Lu Longhouse Café
And was asking him about all the music
That he sang and on piano did play.
In Hawaii he is called "Mr. Maui",
And it's easy to understand why:
His voice is as soft as the Tradewinds,
Yet as strong as a kite flying high,
Reaching up for the clouds, swiftly passing,
In the vibrant and blue Kihei sky
As it touches the soul and the heartstrings
Of those lucky to be passing by.
For the people who listen to Jesse
Are indeed like the clouds up above
Who are touched by his magical singing
That is filled with emotion and love.
And, as they return to their homelands,
They carry a feeling unique
That echoes the heartbeat of Maui:
Jesse gave them what they came to seek!

What impressed me most about Jesse
Was his love for the work that he does
As he talks about why he's performing
And the joy in presenting what was...
In an effort to continue tradition
And present that of which he is proud
In a way that invites us to join him
By singing his message aloud.

There's a beautiful song about weddings
And the tunes telling us where he's at,
And the tender reminders of childhood...
And of weaving a coconut hat.

Here's to Jesse, indeed "Mr. Maui",
May he long bring us moments of joy
As he serenades list'ners with feeling
And reveals what he'd learned as a boy
Growing up on the island of Maui
In a quaint, picturesque whaling town,
Then presenting his shows down in Kihei,
Where he reigns as performer renowned.

Jesse Nakooka reinforced for me the true meaning of "Aloha", continually taking time to greet visitors and to share with pride the history and the culture of his island home of Maui.

Prior to his retirement from his career as a singer, Jesse often appeared, especially during the Christmas holidays, at the Wailea Outrigger Resort. He was accompanied by four local hula performers who added a special "local" touch to his programs. He had many fans from the Mainland—individuals who came back year after year to visit with "Mr. Maui" and to be entertained by his musical talents.

"Mr. Maui", Jesse Nakooka, entertains residents and visitors in Wailea during the holidays, greeting everyone with a smile and with the phrase "Mele Kalikimaka" (Merry Christmas)

When I continue south along Kihei Road, I make a left turn onto Kulanihakoi Road and pay a visit to my friends at the local Episcopal Church. This church has become my spiritual home on the island, and I have become a part of the parish "ohana". After attending a Sunday service here in May of 1997, I was inspired to write a poem about...

Trinity Episcopal Church-by-the-Sea

When you come to the island of Maui
God's presence can be seen everywhere.
But it's not just reflected in Nature,
For its people are willing to share
The magnificent "Spirit of Aloha"
That one feels wherever he goes:
A spirit of friendship and kindness
Which on visitors each resident bestows.

Trinity Episcopal Church-by-the-Sea
Is a place that now lives in my heart
And each time I return to Kihei,
It's a place where my visits I start.
The Spirit of the Lord there surrounds me
As the worshippers greet me with pride,
Inviting me to join them in prayer
Under palm trees and Tradewinds outside.
The multi-cultural parish
Is blessed by the Grace of the Lord;
Parts of services are sung in Hawaiian
As in song He is worshipped and adored.

This church has no roof or side walls:
It is set in a picturesque site.
The palm trees and Tradewinds are ushers
That echo the prayers, day and night...

Each time I return to the Mainland
Part of this church comes along:
Its beautiful Spirit of Aloha—
With such spirit one can never go wrong.

A Sunday service begins at Trinity Episcopal Church-by-the-Sea in Kihei

What a beautiful setting for a church!

Rev. Morley Frech greets a young member of the parish during the Living Nativity Reenactment in December 1997

Ruth Murata-Eisen is the organist and choirmaster at Trinity Episcopal

During the Christmas Season, the parishioners at Trinity-by-the-Sea set up a live nativity on the church grounds, and residents and visitors are invited to share the joy of the season with members of the parish. The church choir performs many of the familiar holiday carols, and at one point during the program, the singing of "Silent Night" is accompanied by a performance of hula. How better to describe this event than with a photo and a poem.

A performance of hula to the carol "Silent Night" adds a special touch to the presentation of the living nativity

The Nativity at Trinity

Every December Christ's birth comes to life
At Trinity Church-by-the-Sea
As parishioners there give THEIR special gift:
A LIVING NATIVITY.

On the second and third Sunday evening,
From seven until eight-thirty each night,
Kihei, on the island of Maui,
Is blessed by this wonderful sight.

The grounds of the Kihei Episcopal Church
Are transformed into Bethlehem's site...
Where shepherds in the fields saw in the sky
The brilliance of that special star's light
That would guide them to the Bethlehem stable
In which our Savior was born...
And there, as He slept in a manger,
Special gifts by the Wise Men were borne.

The choir from the church congregation
Sings carols in praise of the Lord,
While a special performance of hula
Explains why this Child is adored.

Coming back onto South Kihei Road, I need only drive four blocks to reach
the area of Kihei that I call my home away from home...

My home on the island is in Kihei,
It's the Maui Schooner Resort.
From my third-floor lanai
I watch boats passing by
And, at times, humpback whales that cavort,
Breaching in the waters of the Pacific,
Displaying their ability and size...
For those on the shore
Who keep watching for more
As their movements are a joy to our eyes.

Humpback whale surfaces in the waters along the Kihei Coast

The best way to introduce you to this idyllic spot along the Kihei Shores of Maui is with a poem, some photographs, and another poem. The first poem was written in December of 1997; the second in May of 1999. The photos speak for themselves....

The Maui Schooner Resort

I enjoy coming to Maui!
I come three times each year
And travel down to Kihei,
Where the skies are blue and clear.
I have a timeshare unit
That overlooks the sea,
Providing views of sunsets
That set my spirit free.
My resort, The Maui Schooner,
Is a timeshare dream come true:
Each apartment is quite spacious—
With lanai and kitchen, too! —
And offers every owner
A place to feel at ease
While watching as the Tradewinds
The palm trees' fronds do tease.

The grounds of The Maui Schooner
Provide a perfect spot
To watch windsurfers in action
As the surfers' sails are caught
In the ever-changing Tradewinds
Near Maalaea Bay...
You can also watch the humpback whales
Who in winter there will play.

It's a perfect place to fly a kite
On the green and spacious lawn,
Or spend some time at poolside
As each new day does dawn.

294

Kihei's Maui Schooner
Is my home away from home
Each time I come to Maui,
On the Valley Isle to roam.

Building B at the Maui Schooner Resort

A view of the West Maui Mountains from a lanai in Building A

David Geist (left) and two of the resort landscapers greet guests in the Hawaiian style

The pool at the Maui Schooner Resort, facing Building B, June 1994

The Maui Schooner

Have you been to The Maui Schooner
Along the Kihei shores?
If not, you really should do so,
For the views and for oh, so much more!
There are craft classes held on the premises
And tennis and shuffleboard, too;
You can learn about island activities;
There's no limit to what you can do.

The reason I come to the Schooner
Each time that to Maui I fly
Is that there, I can watch Nature's beauty
From a chair on my apartment's lanai...
Enjoying the dances of palm fronds
As they sway in the Tradewinds by day,
Then silently watch as the sun sets,
Like a patron attending a play.

The next time you come down to Kihei
While exploring the great Valley Isle,
Make the Schooner a stop on your journey:
You will no doubt remain for a while.

Each sunset is different and every evening, resort owners and local residents gather along the shoreline to witness the beauty of the display of colors and of the sun's rays reflecting off the water's surface. As the sun sets beneath the horizon, the sound of conch shells being blown resonates through the air, and all along the shoreline torches are lighted, signaling another evening in Paradise.

The Maui Schooner Resort as seen from the resort property just prior to sunset

Sunset along the beach at the Maui Schooner Resort in Kihei

A February sunset at the beach of the Maui Schooner Resort

I am never without my "trusty" Quick-Snap one-time-use flash camera with 800-speed Fujifilm, looking for something unusual that might result in inspiration for a poem. One such inspiration occurred on February 7, 2001, at 7:30 P.M. as I was walking near poolside at the Schooner. The photograph enhanced the literary image I had created, as you will see in my discussion of the...

Torches in the Moonlight

Standing by the Maui Schooner poolside,
I watched the full moon rise
Between two flaming torches:
A marvelous sight for one's eyes.
The flames danced in the Tradewinds,
Surrounding the moon as she rose,
Their fingers touching her surface,
Then retreating—in respect, I suppose.
The brilliance of the moonlight,
Like the beam from a lighthouse tower,
Cast shadows of the flames on the water,
Reflecting their strength and their power.

Within minutes the moon, traveling upward,
Escaped from the grips of the flames...
As their fingers reached up in frustration:
Their success falling short of their aims.
I watched as the torches' reflections
Became smaller as the moon swiftly rose,
Their strength and power diminished,
While the real flames kept their vigilant pose.

I captured the scene with my camera,
Then returned to my Schooner lanai
To wait for the moon, filled with wonder,
As she traveled 'cross the star-studded sky.

The mysterious Torch-Light Hand near the pool of the Maui Schooner tries in vain to catch the full moon as it rises over Kihei on February 7, 2001

I sat on the lanai that evening for hours, mesmerized by the display of stars. (Back in New Jersey, it is rare to see a sky clear enough to reveal the millions and millions of sparkling jewels in the Heavens.) As I watched, I received inspiration from the...

Hawaiian Sky Drama

As I sat out on the lanai
Of my Maui island suite
Watching moonset over Kihei—
The day's last brilliant feat—
I stared into the heavens,
Where the twinkling stars abound,
And thought I heard them speaking...
Though I couldn't hear a sound.
For the sky was like a backdrop
Used as setting for a play,
And the stars the budding actors
Putting on their proud display...
Of outfits gleaming in the lights,
Of voices taut with fear
In great anticipation
Of the audience's cheer.

But were those stars just bits of light
Twinkling in the skies?
Or were they spirits so sublime
Which, with winking of their eyes,
Encourage me to wonder
And to dream away my cares?
And even offer challenges,
Or, perhaps, just answer prayers?

The moonset now completed,
I returned to solid ground
And marveled at the feelings
Which in their play I'd found.
And, as I left the lanai,
I glanced once more above
To watch those actors winking
From their wondrous Stage of Love.

Early in 1991, I went to my travel agent to make arrangements for a flight to Maui for the week of the eighth to the fifteenth of July. I had already requested that week at the Schooner, and my mom and I were looking forward to the trip. We almost didn't make it, however, since most flights to the Hawaiian Islands that week were fully booked. I didn't know until I arrived on the island that a very special celestial event was scheduled to occur in the skies over Maui on Thursday, July 11: a total eclipse of the sun. "Eclipse-watchers" from all around the world had gathered on Maui for this spectacular event. I was very excited and woke up VERY early that morning so that I, too, could be an eye-witness to...

The Solar Eclipse of 1991

On the island of Maui, on the eleventh of July,
An event long-predicted took place in the sky...
As the moon showed its power by eclipsing the sun,
Turning daylight to twilight before it was done!
But for those who had waited to view the great sight,
Many dreams turned to nightmares during "dawn's early light"...

For the two-hour program, prearranged for us all,
Was kept hidden by Ma Nature, who arranged for a squall!
There were clouds and thick fog all over the isle,
So that no one could see IT, not even for a while.
The eclipse was detected by a darkening sky,
But the moon's great performance wasn't seen by the eye!

I was there when it happened: I was out on a boat...
Getting drenched by the downpour, trying hard not to gloat.
For I'd sensed what was happening as the temperature dropped...
And an eerie gray color proved that sunlight had stopped!
I was thrilled by the moment, I and twenty-three more
Who, with Bruce, Buck, and Kelly, tried the gods to implore
To provide us with a "window" through which we might see
The sun's bright corona from our seats on the sea!
We prepared our sunpeepers and drank some champagne,
While enjoying our "fieldtrip" in the wind and the rain.
I shall never forget it! What more can I say?
For although I saw nothing, I enjoyed the whole day!

TOTAL ECLIPSE

The Great Hawaiian Eclipse

I still enjoy watching the videotape that I made that morning, as twenty-four excited visitors shared a special adventure in the waters off the Kihei coast of Maui. The captain of the vessel that had been reserved for our group said that, in his twenty-five years as a captain of cruises and special events along the Maui coast, he had never seen such an incredible display of bad weather.

Later that day, I watched news reports from Honolulu on TV and video-taped the eclipse from one news report. The ONLY island affected by the stormy weather on July 11, 1991, was the island of Maui—the island from which views of the total solar eclipse were anticipated.

Dining in Maui is often much more than just a treat for the taste buds; it offers scenic views of the beaches and of tropical landscapes, as well as encounters with many of the local birds, who do not hesitate to stop by and check out the menu and, of course, feast on any crumbs found under the tables. One of these dining experiences revealed to me—and to the birds....

An Invisible Danger

I was seated in Sunsets at the Beach,
The waves from the ocean in easy reach.
The meal I was eating was really a treat:
Pineapple pizza! It just can't be beat!
'Twas December 13 in the year '94,
To the island of Maui I had come to explore
And escape from the snow and the cold arctic air
That was threatening New Jersey and, of course, Delaware.

The walls of this restaurant were all made of glass
On the ocean and poolsides, so that Tradewinds could pass
And add to the beauty of this oceanfront site:
It made beachfront dining a diner's delight!
Because of the noise of the crowds at the pool,
Those accordion-style windows were kept closed as a rule...
While those on the oceanside were kept open wide
So that diners could enjoy all the sounds from outside.

As the diners enjoyed all the Maui-style treats,
Birds from the island would fly in and take seats
On the floor of the restaurant, awaiting a chance
On stray bits of food from the tables to prance.

Two diners had come in and were seated for lunch
At a quaint corner table, and had ordered some punch
When suddenly they screamed and decided to move
To another small table... but why did they move?
Two frolicking birds had come flying along
And found that their eyesight had guided them wrong:
As they flew through the wide-open oceanside wall,
They collided, head-on, with the poolside glass wall...
And dropped to the floor with an ominous thud,
Just like rooftops collapsing in the wake of a flood.
The two little bodies lay lifeless and limp,
The result of the contact with the "invisible imp"...
Those solid-glass panels that appeared to be air,
But, indeed, were a threat to those unaware
Of the invisible danger just lying in wait—
Like the worm that the fisherman uses for bait—
For innocent victims who couldn't foresee
What results from attempts to fly through them would be!

I'm happy to say that the birds did survive,
Though at first they DID seem more dead than alive,
And finally flew off to safer terrain.
But will they remember not to come there again?

The moral that comes from this near tragedy
Is really quite simple, as you will now see:
Be careful whenever you travel in haste
For in time and in suffering, "Haste indeed will make waste!"

During another dining experience, my powers of observation, combined with a somewhat vivid imagination, gave me an idea of how one species of birds got its yellow beak. From that 1997 experience came a poem that explains why, whenever I see this bird...

I Call Him "Butter Beak"

Have you ever seen a Mina Bird?
It truly is unique...
For tho' its body's mostly black,
It has a yellow beak.
If you ask an ornathologist
About its beak so bright,
The answer you'll be given
Will fill you with delight:
By tracing genealogy,
Geography and more,
The history of the "Mina Bird"
Will help you "know the score".

I'm not an ornathologist,
But I think that *I* know why
Its beak is brilliant yellow,
For I've looked it in the eye
And have watched its daily habits
On Hawaii's Valley Isle:
From all MY observations,
Here's the evidence in my file...

While sitting in a restaurant
At the Aston Wailea Resort,
Enjoying a buffet breakfast,
I wrote this true report...

A Mina Bird came flying in,
For it was hungry, too,
And spied an empty table,
With just a plate or two!
The customers had eaten
Almost ev'rything in sight—
The only "food" remaining
Was something smooth and bright
That was served with sev'ral pancakes...
But only some remained.

The Mina Bird took careful aim
(It looked like it was trained!)
And, landing on the table,
Immersed its eager beak
Into the cup of butter:
I didn't dare to speak.

What happened next convinced me
That MY research would prove
Why Mina Birds have yellow beaks,
For how that bird did move!
It flew out to the railing
And, with an artist's skill,
Began to spread the butter
On both sides of its "bill".
It tried so hard to wipe it off,
But it would not let go...
And so, as everyone could see,
That beak was now aglow.

In search of needed nourishment,
The Mina Bird obtained
That brilliant yellow color
On its beak... that has remained
As ev'ry generation
Accepted this technique...

And now YOU know the reason
Why *I* call him "Butter Beak".

With this poem, I have reached the area of Wailea on the trip south along Kihei Road. The Wailea area on the island has grown in the past twenty years, with a number of resort hotel complexes offering spectacular views of Paradise, both natural and manmade. My island poetry friend Diana Stuart introduced me to one such resort in 1996: a complex located on a hillside overlooking the waters of Wailea known as...

The entrance to the Diamond Resort overlooking the Wailea area of the island

The Diamond Resort:
A Picturesque Setting

I was sitting at the beautiful Diamond Resort,
On a bench overlooking the falls.
With my eyes closed, I was listening to Nature
As the Tradewinds caressed the rock walls.
In the distance, the raindrops were falling
Up in Kula, not too far away,
As both horses and cattle kept grazing
On the slopes, as they do every day.

My thoughts were in flight with those Tradewinds
O'er the brilliant blue waters below,
Envisioning a spiritual Paradise
Enhanced by the tide's ebb and flow.
My senses reached out in excitement
To smell, touch, and hear this new world
Which, released by the absence of vision,
Came alive and, like a flag, was unfurled.

The scent of tropical flowers
Brought to mind wond'rous visions of love,
While the touch of the Tradewinds, like dewdrops,
Conjured up scenes of peace from Above.
The sound of the cascading waters,
Dancing proudly on the shimmering rocks,
Conveyed scenes of picturesque beauty—
In *this* world, there was no need for clocks.

As I opened my eyes, I was greeted
By a gecko who was looking my way
From the palm fronds overlooking the beauty:
He smiled, and then scurried away.
On the lawn of a neighboring hillside
A heron was strutting along.
As I watched her, I listened intently...
For it seemed she was singing a song.

The sun, in magnificent splendor,
Was at play on Haleakala's slopes,
Painting picturesque scenes of shadow and light—
As one's mind paints frustrations and hopes.

I spent half a day at the Diamond Resort
On the hills close to Kihei's south shore,
And, as I departed to catch my flight,
I knew that I'd come back for more.

A view of the waterfall at the Diamond Resort, as seen from the registration area

A view of the waterfall from the benches located near the restaurant of the Diamond Resort

Looking toward the Upcountry area of Maui from the reception area of the Diamond Resort

Another talented entertainer who came to Maui for the first time in the late 1970s is Mr. Tony Van Steen. He combines careers in music and in sports in a way that amazes most people who hear about him or see him in action—on the tennis court or at the piano keyboard. I found an article in the April 20 - 26, 2000 issue of the *Maui Island Weekly* that I feel is a good way for me to introduce Tony to you. The article, entitled "Simple Announcement, Simple Story, Quite a Guy", written by Joseph Sugarman, includes the following information:

> *When Tony first arrived here on Maui from San Diego over 20 years ago, he got a job as a security guard at what was then called the Wailea Beach Hotel. It was a good job and Tony, a former soldier in the Dutch Navy, had the strength and size to nicely fill his post. At least everybody thought so.*
>
> *Then came the hurricane of 1980 that struck Maui and stranded a group of musicians who were playing at the resort. The resort management needed somebody to at least play the piano for the guests who were waiting out the storm at the hotel. The management noticed that Tony, who had only worked for three weeks at the resort, had written on his job description that he played the piano. They asked him if he could perform for the guests. He agreed...*
>
> *The storm blew over in four days, but Tony kept playing long after the hurricane passed. Months went into years and years passed quickly. The hotel soon changed its name to the Stouffer Wailea Resort... and Tony continued to play.*
>
> *Thirteen years later, Tony was still playing, never to see his security job again....*

My mother and I first met Tony at a Sunday breakfast buffet at the Raffles Restaurant in the Stouffer Wailea Resort, in the summer of 1991. I made a special request of Tony that morning: I asked him to perform the tune "Spanish Eyes" for my mom. (Remember... I was a career Spanish teacher!) We thanked him for his kindness before leaving the restaurant.

The next summer, I once again brought Mom to Maui for a week of relaxation, and on Sunday morning, we returned to Raffles for the breakfast buffet. When Tony saw us enter the restaurant, he interrupted the tune he was playing and serenaded us with "Spanish Eyes". WOW! Needless to say, we have been friends ever since, and I visit him up in Maui Meadows during each trip to Maui.

When I came to Maui in February of 2003, Tony, now eighty-four years young, greeted me in typical style: As he saw me drive up and park by his tennis courts, he went to his keyboard and began playing "Spanish Eyes". How is that for the "Spirit of Aloha"!

The April 2000 newspaper article did include one comment from Tony: "You never know what life has in store." My experiences during the past decade reflect that statement beautifully. When I decided to take an early retirement from my position as a Spanish instructor—at the young age of forty-nine—my friends and colleagues said I was making a BIG mistake, that I would become bored with retirement within six to eight months and I would be back in the classroom as a substitute within a year. I had no idea about "what life had in store for me", but a request from Mr. Bill Westphal, the principal of my alma mater, Audubon High School, for a copy of a poem I had composed about the patriotic achievements of the AHS students turned out to be like the request from the hotel management to Tony Van Steen to play the piano.... I have been writing ever since. Here is my special...

Tribute to Mr. Tony Van Steen

There once was a man in Hawaii
Who entertained guests while they ate.
He played the requests
Of all of his guests...
And his playing was really "first rate"!

His friends, they all knew him as "Tony",
Tho' his full name is Tony Van Steen.
He played at his best,
And never would rest
While the diners enjoyed the cuisine.
Tony played the piano at Raffles
Every Sunday at a scrumptious buffet...
And once ev'ry year
Mom and I would appear
Just to listen to him as he'd play.

I taught Spanish in the state of New Jersey,
In a high school named Cherry Hill EAST,
And each time that we came
OUR request was the same:
"Spanish Eyes" gave our ears a great feast!

But wait! There's more you should know about Tony,
For he's famous on Maui these days
For his work on the courts,
Playing tennis in shorts,
Giving lessons that result in much praise!

For you see, he ENJOYS playing tennis
And instructs in a marvelous way:
He will never act mean
And will not cause a scene,
As his students improve in their play!

He approaches the game with enjoyment
And finds humor his very best friend:
To encourage a smile
While improving in style...
With fantastic results in the end,
Since his students react to his comments
By working very hard to improve.
And their progress relies
On those great mental "highs"
That result from their "finding the groove"
In their serve, as they pay strict attention
To position of racquet and wrist—
And in backhand technique
Which improves ev'ry week
As the ball on the "sweet spot" is kissed!
For the students no longer keep trying
To swing just as hard as can be...
And, to their delight,
The ball, once in flight,
Doesn't head for the airport, you see.

Coach Tony Van Steen is the reason
Why success has been coming their way!
They have learned how to smile...
While perfecting their style...
And enjoy each set that they play!

Tony tickles the iv'ries by moonlight;
Plays the net on the court every day.
And wherever he plays
He has shown that it pays
To enjoy what you do and you say...

For his songs bring delight to his list'ners
And his words... they convey what they mean.
So all over the isle,
There is always a smile
When one talks about Tony Van Steen.

THANK YOU, Tony, for all you have given
To visitors and friends ev'ry year.
Both at home and away
Those who know you will say:
"Let's give Tony an appreciative cheer!"

Just keep doing what makes you feel happy,
For it's what makes US happy as well.
Make us smile while we eat,
Or while moving our feet
On the court: The results have been swell!

Tony Van Steen
Eighty-one and looking like a young man

Tony Van Steen entertaining diners at Raffles Restaurant

On December 22, 1998, Tony Van Steen celebrated his eightieth birthday. I was honored when I received an invitation from Tony to come to his big celebration on the island of Maui. What a day! Guests were in attendance from all around the world—from Europe, from the Mainland and, of course, from the islands, including many of his tennis students. I present the following set of photos, knowing that you will feel the "Aloha" spirit that was present...

Photo by Lynnie Marie

Tony Van Steen greets guests to his Maui Meadows home

Tony and his wife Harriet share an Aloha smile with friends in San Diego in 1999

While on Maui in early September of 2001 to attend the Maui Writers' Conference, I took time to stop by for a visit with Tony, only to find...

Tony on the Mend

I went to see Tony Van Steen today...
And waited 'til late afternoon:
He'd be out on the tennis courts with students by four
And I didn't want to get there too soon.
I arrived at his home on Mapu Place
And must admit I was somewhat surprised:
No cars were parked on the street by the courts.
No lessons, due to heat, I surmised.

When I walked up the steps to the second deck,
I heard Tony say: "Come on in."
What is this? Van Steen on the sofa?
How odd! But he said, with a grin...
"I was in San Diego in August
When suddenly, I became rather ill:
A tumor as large as a tennis ball was found
In my colon—and removed with great skill.
'The tumor is malignant', said the surgeon,
'But very little of the cancer has spread.
You may not require chemotherapy...
You're quite lucky: You could now be dead.'

"Sooo... Here I am, resting in comfort,
Feeling better, but counting the hours
'Til I once again find myself back on the courts,
Giving lessons, not smelling the flowers."

At age eighty-two, this remarkable man
Continues to amaze all his friends,
Teaching tennis and "tickling the ivories"...
Thus, as his stitched abdomen mends,
He'll once again take on the challenge
Of an active and creative routine,
Providing excitement and pleasure.
He's our champion: Tony Van Steen!

322

Tony Van Steen passed away in December 2005 from liver cancer. Beginning in January of 2006, an annual invitational tennis tournament, named in Tony's memory, is held in Wailea.

Another delightful location for dining on Maui is located on the Gold Course of the golf complex in Wailea. It is another picturesque spot on the island introduced to me by Diana Stuart. The SeaWatch Restaurant was the site of the 2002 Senior Skins Game. When a customer is served coffee in this restaurant, it comes in a cup that is as large as a soup bowl. The cup is greenish-blue in color, to match nature's beauty in the surrounding hillsides. This location was the inspiration for my poem about the birds that were following the lawnmower that appeared in the introduction. Of course, it is also the inspiration for another poem, simply titled...

The SeaWatch Restaurant: A Special Dining Experience

Whenever I come to Maui,
No matter how long the stay,
I visit the SeaWatch Restaurant:
What a great way to start your day!
Should I come on Sunday or Thursday,
I'm greeted in Aloha-style
By Skipper, the hostess on duty:
She always is wearing a smile.
Skipper and all the employees
Make dining at the SeaWatch a joy.
They all are a perfect reflection
Of the motto: "Maui No Ka Oi".
Come to SeaWatch in scenic Wailea,
You'll enjoy both the food and the views:
From omelettes to sandwiches to dinners;
From Molokini to great sunset hues.

Molokini is the crescent-shaped island to which many snorkelers and scuba-divers come every day. The underwater views of coral and of the native fish are remarkable, and the waters are so clear that the fish can be seen from the deck of the boats that run excursions to this island from Maalaea Harbor.

On one of my visits to the SeaWatch in Wailea, I met a lady who serves as hostess several mornings each week. I learned that she also is a talented dancer and dance instructor who offers classes at the Arts and Cultural Center for residents old and young. Her love of life and her desire to share the joy of dancing inspired my poetic salute to...

Skipper Smith:
A Dancer with a Heart of Gold

At the Maui Arts and Cultural Center
One will find a school of dance,
With classes taught by Skipper Smith:
Stop in, should you get the chance.
What you'll see is a talented instructor
Whose students will always recall
The 2000 Sydney Olympics...
And the performance at Carnegie Hall.

Skipper's love for dancing is evident
As she works with the youth on the isle,
Encouraging in them self-confidence
As they learn to perform with a smile.

Skipper came to the island of Maui
In September of nineteen ninety-eight
To become a full-time resident—
And instructor who is truly first rate.
She began her career as a teacher:
As assistant at the age of fifteen.
Now, only fifty-nine years later,
Her students still perform "on the scene".

The owners of the Norwegian Cruise Lines
Have invited her students to perform
On a June 2002 voyage:
Not many these days get the chance

To perform for an international audience,
Displaying both technique and grace,
To jazz, ballet, and tap numbers.
Thanks to Skipper, such performances take place.

Skipper worked in a unique pilot program
Which the government had established in dance:
A program for handicapped children.
Her students, with joy, did advance
As they worked together with Skipper,
Who encouraged them on to success.
They learned that, in spite of their handicaps,
They could perform at their best, nothing less.

Skipper Smith is a Maui Isle treasure
And a talent who will never grow old,
For she shares her love with others:
She's a dancer with a heart of gold.

I have taken you to nearly every scenic spot on the island. Now I want to share with you some of the experiences I have had over the years: with the people, with Nature, and with special events in which I have been fortunate enough to participate.

I begin with a poem written at the Maui Schooner, following a hula presentation by some of the young local students. Their presentation helped me to learn and appreciate...

Maui Movements

Native performers,
Proud of their rich heritage,
Help traditions live.

Young hula dancers,
Dressed in colorful attire,
Dance with hips and hands.

Gently swaying hips,
Combined with silent language
Of the dancers' hands,
Beckon us to watch
As history comes alive
In Maui movements.

Older performers
Translate every movement;
Help us understand.

Let's understand them
And learn—from Maui movements—
How history lives!

Young hula dancers perform for visitors on the grounds of the Maui Schooner Resort in Kihei

Young Hawaiians from a cultural dance studio perform for participants in the 2002 Maui Writers' Conference on a stage at the Wailea Marriott Resort

One of the resorts in the Wailea area of Maui is the Wailea Marriott, home since 2000 of the Annual Maui Writers' Conference. I attended my first conference in 1995 and then returned in 2000, when I had a chance to show author Jack Canfield my book on patriotism. I was both surprised and excited when Mr. Canfield agreed to have a photo taken with me. When I returned in 2001, Canfield, the now co-author of *Chicken Soup for the Veteran's Soul*, agreed to write an endorsement for my book! Because of his kindness—and the show of Aloha by all of the organizers of the conference—I sponsored three teachers and two students to the 2002 conference so that they could have a chance to experience what I had over the past six years. The student from Audubon High School, Tara Conte, entered a short story entitled "The Legend of Mr. Warble" in the Young Writers' Competition. WOW! On Friday evening, the winners of the student competition were announced, and Tara had won the top prize. On Saturday morning, she was interviewed on a local TV station on Maui. Back in Audubon, Tara was honored by the Board of Education for her accomplishment. Needless to say, I was a very proud sponsor! Here is a photo collage that reflects my experiences at the Maui Writers' Conference....

Above: Maui Writers' Conference Chairpersons John and Shannon Tullius welcome participants to the opening session

Conference hostess, guest speaker, and Author Sam Horn greets participants prior to her workshop on the craft of writing

Above: 2002 Young Writers' Competition Short Story Top Prize Winner Tara Conte from Audubon High School in Audubon, New Jersey, poses with AHS faculty members Brian Kulak and John Skrabonja after the Awards Ceremony

Tara Conte is interviewed by a TV station on Maui and discusses what inspired her short story: "The Legend of Mr. Warble"

When I attended the conference in 2001, I stayed in Room 7204, with a view toward the ocean. Right outside my room, two native trees were growing and their "embrace" inspired me to write about...

An Expression of Love in Paradise

They grew up as friends and neighbors
At the Wailea Marriott Resort...
Then, during adolescence, went off in search
Of adventure, on trips long and short.
But true love brought them together again
And now, as they fondly embrace,
They recall all the changes in the neighborhood—
Known as progress in the world's human race.

As they dance in the afternoon Tradewinds,
Awaiting glorious sunsets,
These two trees grow old with great pleasure:
For them, there can be no regrets.

Continuing south from Wailea, the visitor reaches the area of Makena. This section of Maui contains a number of beaches, as well as a church with a marvelous history, located right along the shoreline and with a cemetery on the church grounds. In several locations, water can be seen shooting into the air from blowholes in the lava rock along the beaches, as the tide comes in. Once again, a photo is worth at least a thousand words....

Patriotism on the 50th State

SOME THOUGHTS AND VIEWS OF
THE RESPONSE OF RESIDENTS
OF MAUI TO THE TERRORIST
ATTACKS ON SEPT. 11, 2001

Sign on the side of a bus bringing tourists to the Kaanapali Station of
the Sugarcane Train on February 21, 2003, reflects the patriotism of the
Hawaiian people

As I stated earlier, I am the liaison from Audubon, New Jersey, to the U.S. Navy and to the officers and crew of the USS *Benfold* (DDG-65). In early September 2001, I traveled to Pearl Harbor to greet the crew of the ship as she pulled into the harbor after a six-month deployment in the Arabian Gulf region. After greeting the ship, I returned to Maui for a five-day stay prior to flying to San Diego, California, where I would greet the ship again.

Little did I know what was to happen on Tuesday, September 11, just a day before I was to fly from Kahului to San Diego. The tragic event of that day kept me on Maui until Saturday, September 15. I composed three poems, the first in which I described…

The Day the World Trade Center Died

I was on the island of Maui
September eleventh, two thousand one—
My second home, in Paradise,
Relaxing 'neath the tropical sun.

At 8:46 in the morning
Diana Stuart, a friend on the isle,
Called me at the Maui Schooner Resort:
What she told me wiped away the relaxed smile.
"Did you wake up? Have you heard the news?
You'd better turn your TV set on!
The World Trade Center has been destroyed
And terrorists damaged the Pentagon!"

Every channel was covering the event.
It was something quite hard to believe:
Commercial airline flights had been hijacked.
What devastation each plane did leave!
Two crashed into the World Trade Center;
A third into the Pentagon.
The Twin Towers then completely collapsed:
One-fifth of the Pentagon was gone.

The first crash occurred at 8:46 A.M.,
The second at 9:05 Eastern Time.
Fires were spreading out of control...
Who was behind such a crime?

All commercial airline flights
Have been cancelled 'til September twelfth, at noon.
President Bush, who was in Florida,
Will address the nation quite soon.

America was severely wounded today,
As on December seventh, nineteen forty-one.
I was not yet born on THAT date,
But have firsthand knowledge of THIS one.

What makes today's news so eerie for me,
On a day I shall never forget,
Is that just last Wednesday, September the fifth,
I flew to Pearl Harbor by jet:
Went aboard the USS *Arizona*;
Said a prayer for all those who were lost.
Now, sixty years later, I can only guess
At what the September eleventh tragedy will cost....

When Diana called me that morning, it was already 2:46 P.M. in New York City. As a result, I saw and heard within a span of about five minutes what had taken nearly two and a half hours to take place. As I learned more and more about the events of that day, I was inspired to compose a second poem, which was written on September 13. Perhaps the fact that I was on the island of Maui inspired me to include several local references in the selection...

America under Attack:

September 11, 2001

It began in New York City
On a sunny Tuesday morn:
In the World Trade Center Twin Towers
Two fiery blossoms were born
That bloomed in the Manhattan skyline,
Erupting in a ghastly display...
Then collapsing, and dying within hours,
Covered in remains ashen gray.

348

These blossoms, just like the Silversword plant
On Maui, took thirty years to mature:
Two 110-story structures,
Stately stems with a silent allure.
The roots of these Manhattan giants
Had trembled in nineteen ninety-three
When a plot to destroy these magnificent twins
Failed to achieve victory.
Eight years later, on September eleventh
In the year two thousand one,
A second terrorist plot succeeded...
Thus, their three-decade lifespan was done.

Like bumblebees searching for pollen,
Hijacked aircraft flew into the Towers.
Within seconds, fireball blossoms appeared,
Blooming in lava-like showers
Of metal and concrete and human remains,
Falling to the sidewalks below,
Followed by the total collapse of the stems...
That for days continued to glow.

Two other airliners, like killer bees,
Buzzed through the skies that day:
One attacking our country's Pentagon;
A second (Destination? Who could say?)
Crash-landing in Pennsylvania
Before ever reaching its goal.
Four airplanes, filled with civilians,
Who added to the total death toll.

Two days later, ten other terrorists
Were arrested while boarding two planes—
At LaGuardia and JFK Airports.
Where would these "bees" have left more bloodstains?

America's colors bloomed brightly that month
In vivid Red, White, and Blue
As citizens everywhere came to the aid
Of victims whom few of them knew.

Patriotism triumphed over terrorism
In September, two thousand one.
Although the nation was injured severely,
It will heal, as it always has done.

I was witness to a wonderful display of patriotism on the island of Maui during my four-day extended stay. What I saw not only made me proud to be an American but also thankful that I had been given a chance to be on the island that week and to observe flags flying everywhere. I took one photo from the parking lot at 501 Front Street in Lahaina, showing flags flying from every light standard and telephone pole along the street....

My experiences inspired a third poem, with a focus on...

The Aftermath of Tragedy: Patriotism on Maui

In our fiftieth state, Hawaii,
On Maui, the Valley Isle,
A wonderful display of patriotism
Was evident (there was no denial)
In schools, in newspapers,
On radio station KPOA
As local residents showed their pride
In a sincere and caring way
Following the unforeseen terrorist attacks
In New York City and in Washington, D.C.
I witnessed this local display firsthand:
What wonderful images I did see.

Radio Station KPOA,
Ninety-three-point-five, FM,
Interrupted regular programming
On September twelfth, twelve P.M.
For a moment of prayer and silence
For those who had lost their lives
At the World Trade Center and the Pentagon—
Sons, daughters, husbands, and wives.

A special memorial service
Was held on the Ceremonial Green
Of the Arts and Cultural Center.
Everywhere flags could be seen!

At the Maui Marketplace Office Max
The customers who entered the store
Were given a sticker of the American Flag
To wear as they walked out the door.

353

In schools all over the island
On Friday, the National Day of Prayer,
School bands played "The Star-Spangled Banner":
True patriotic pride filled the air.
Principals and students held assemblies that day
To remember the tragic event,
All wearing Red, White, and Blue ribbons:
Love and caring were quite evident.

On Friday, at noon, a service was held
At Trinity Episcopal Church-by-the-Sea:
Just one of many island church services held,
Focusing on spirituality.

In its Saturday edition, *The Maui News*
Published, on a full page, with pride,
A full-color replica of the American Flag:
A fine tribute to those who had died.

Mahalo nui loa, residents of Maui,
Your images helped me deal with our loss.
Your Spirit of Aloha shown brightly that week,
Reflected well—in the flag and the cross.

I left Maui at 10:00 P.M. on September 15, 2001. I then returned in February
of 2002, only to discover that the flags were still flying proudly everywhere on
the island. As the visitors drove from the airport, they were greeted by a big
sign, thanking them for visiting Maui—and thanks for continuing to FLY, in
spite of the air terrorism of Tuesday, September 11, 2001....

I then drove to my "home away from home," the Maui Schooner Resort, located at 980 South Kihei Road. That first night, I went out for dinner and, upon my return, was greeted by a beautiful display on the roof of one of the local residences: The home at 983 South Kihei Road had an American Flag, constructed of tiny lights in red, white, and blue, shining brightly in the night sky. Curiosity got the best of me, and the following evening, I went across the street from the resort, knocked on the door, and asked for some information about the unique flag. The gentleman who answered the door was Albert Franco, a man of Portuguese descent who is proud to be an American. What he told me brought tears to my eyes and pride to my entire being: The electric flag contains one light for every individual who died as a result of the September 11, 2001, terrorist attacks on New York City and on Washington, D.C. Mr. Franco told me that *The Maui Weekly*, now a bi-monthly publication, was planning a story on his patriotism in its next issue. In the February 21 - March 6, 2002, issue, Mr. Franco's picture appeared, along with the article "Kihei's Electric Flag". Below is that photo; on the next page are two photos I took of the flag: one in the daytime, one at night.

The article included the following comments:

Drive down S. Kihei Road any evening and you'll come across a big new American flag. It's an electric flag, six by ten feet in size and built to the accurate proportions by local electrician Darren Franco. His father, Albert Franco, who came up with the idea for the flag, said the flag will blaze red, white and blue every night from dusk to midnight from the family's roof top "until the war on terrorism is over."

Albert realizes that may be a while, said son Darren. "It's my dad's way of showing support for his beloved country."

Members of the Franco family first arrived in Hawaii in 1883 on the S.S. Hankow. *Darren Franco said he has at least 300 relatives on Maui, and that he keeps running into first cousins he didn't know he had. Last time they had a family reunion, four years ago, 400 relatives came, many from off-island. That 400 represents just a tiny representation of the more than 1,500 relatives they have world-wide.*

What a wonderful show of patriotism! And thank you, Mr. Franco, for talking with me about this special effort in flying our nation's flag!

Author Burgess at the Keauhou Beach Resort in Kailua-Kona, Hawaii, at sunset on Friday, August 15, 2003

Some Closing Thoughts and Images

As I bring to a close my "Fleeting Glimpse of Paradise", I want to share several more thoughts with you. First, an hourglass descriptive poem of...

Maui

Clear
Blue skies
Swaying palms
Cooling Tradewinds
Agile windsurfers
Frisbee tossers
Kite flyers
Lanais
Peace

Bright
Sunshine
Moonlit nights
Fragrant flowers
Flowing waterfalls
Cooling mai tais
Paradise
Maui
Isle

The beauty of the islands continues to attract me, and I spend at least four weeks each year investigating new places and meeting new people. Nevertheless, I have become aware, over the past three decades, of some of the many changes in scenery.

Changes in Paradise

In my forty-one trips to Hawaii
In the past thirty-one years,
I've witnessed a great many changes:
Changes to the eyes and the ears.
Highway construction is constant,
Yet traffic doesn't seem to improve:
As more and more lights are installed,
At times, your car hardly moves.
New homes appear on the horizon
Which limit magnificent views:
Of beaches and palm tree-lined landscapes
With flowers of various hues....

Expansion of highway and installation of traffic lights, eliminating part of a sugarcane field near Kahului, Maui: February 2003

Construction of new ocean-view homes in the Makena area of Maui: February 2003

Sections of new pre-fab housing units in Kihei, Maui: February 2003

Final stages of construction of pre-fab metal housing units in Kihei, Maui, across the street from the New Safeway Supermarket: February 2003

On Thursday, January 2, 2003, an article appeared in the Orange County Edition of the *Los Angeles Times*, written by *Times* Staff Reporter Gary Polakovic and entitled: "Paradise Losing in Hawaii." The subtitle is: "Alien species have altered the archipelago's very nature. Islanders are struggling to save what native plants and animals they still can." I am including several excerpts from this article....

> *...Today, Hawaii—the real Hawaii—is disappearing, its natural and wild character eroding bit by bit each year.*
>
> *Increased tourism, military activity and global trade opened the door to opportunistic invaders—foreign plants and animals—long held at bay by the broad Pacific. The alien species are turning Hawaii's environment upside down. ...*
>
> *But Hawaiians are not just standing by idly, waiting for the next exotic snake or house plant to push on to their shores.*
>
> *Alarmed at the threat to Hawaii's tourism, agriculture and ambiance, scientists, government officials and everyday Hawaiians—from schoolchildren to hoteliers—are waging a multi-front war to save native plants and animals.*
>
> *One Indiana Jones-style "human pollinator" has even gained minor cult status, traipsing from one island to the next—where he climbs trees and rappels down cliffs to dispense pollen once spread by birds and bees." (This modern-day Johnny Pineappleseed," Ken Wood, a federal biologist based on the island of Kauai, hikes to remote areas to gather materials to help in propagation and research on endangered species.)*

The article lists some of the problems seen in the Islands in recent years and talks about the many ways in which Hawaiians are working to restore the natural beauty of the archipelago. As writer Polakovic says in a second subtitle to his article: "Hawaiians Fight to Regain the Paradise They've Lost."

I found this article very interesting, especially because, as I worked on the layout for this book, I included some comments about this very topic. I pointed out that, as civilization encroaches more and more into territory once considered off limits to humans, I often wonder whether the native animals and birds know that efforts are being made to preserve some areas for their use. And so, each time I observe a new shopping center, a new housing development, or a widening of a highway, it brings to mind the poem that I composed....

A Maui Lover's Dream

If only I could someday learn
The language of the birds,
Or memorize the cattle's song
While resting with the herds,
My future lines of poetry
Would paint idyllic scenes,
Enhanced with special metaphors
Mixed in with blues and greens...
For while observing birds and cows
On Hawaii's Valley Isle,
My senses reach out, longing for
What makes these creatures smile.

The palm trees are their landing fields
And serve as lookout sites
From which to view the majesty
Of Maui's days and nights;
The lava rocks and sugarcane
Surround their pasturelands,
Presenting changing sights and sounds
Composed by God's great hands.

These images in Nature's realm
Man's language can't describe:
It's limited by human minds
Which set patterns do describe.
To have a chance to talk and sing
With Maui's wildlife friends
Would open up a wondrous world,
Devoid of fads and trends...
Until that special time arrives,
One promise I shall keep:
I'll not destroy that pristine land
On which its wildlife sleep.

And when I've shared my lifelong dream
With those who don't yet see
That Maui won't be Paradise
For folks like you and me
If, through the years, we build and build,
Ignoring Nature's realm
Until the Valley Isle becomes
Some businessperson's realm...

Perhaps the wildlife on the isle
Will come to me and say:
"Mahalo nui loa, friend!
We'll start teaching you today."

I composed that poem in May of 1999, somewhat concerned at that point of the changes that were occurring on the island. I was happy to learn that efforts are indeed being made to preserve native plants and animals and to find ways to help stabilize the ecology on the islands.

The following photos show why I feel it is important that the state of Hawaii continue to offer a Paradise to visitors from the Mainland....

In 1984, following my second week-long visit to the island of Maui, I composed the poem whose title became the title of this collection of poems and photos....

A Fleeting Glimpse of Paradise

Oh, to be a cirrus cloud
Above the Maui cane,
Floating, oh, so softly,
So near the Kihei plain
Amidst the gently blowing palms
Which grow and sway with ease...
In air that's swept by Tradewinds
Which all their fronds do tease.

My life would be so carefree
As I floated to and fro,
Just puffing up from time to time
As near the hills I'd go.
And though my life would be quite brief
In the sunlit Maui skies,
I'd vanish quite contentedly,
No sadness in my eyes,
And fall upon the Kihei coast
As sweet pineapple rain...
For I'd have been a cirrus cloud
Above the Maui cane!

This poem was the beginning of my career as a poet and the rest, as they say, is history. Positive feedback from this poem encouraged me to write about my experiences in Hawaii over the past two decades.

As you reach the end of my "Fleeting Glimpse of Paradise", know that I shall continue to call Maui my home away from home. And, eventually, more than just my mind will be in the clouds, floating over the sugarcane fields close to the Kihei coast. One of my friends already believes this. After returning from a recent trip that he made with me, when someone asked him, "Where is Craig?" all he could say was, "Craig? Oh, I guess I could say that he's...

Here Today, Gone to Maui

I love the Hawaiian Islands,
And Maui is the best!
The last time on the Valley Isle,
I took along a guest.
We saw the Iao Valley,
Went to Mama's Fish House, too.
On the final day of the visit
It was Lahaina we traveled to.
I sat down on a wooden bench
In quaint Lahaina town,
Set my suitcase down beside me,
Then began to look around.
My friend walked on down Front Street
And into the Pioneer Inn
To do some last-minute shopping:
I just sat there with a grin....
My senses were invaded
By the smells and sounds and sights
Of pineapples, of waves, of rainbows;
Of sugarcane, Tradewinds, and kites.

Artists of all ages
Sat beneath the huge banyan tree,
Painting scenes of Paradise
From the mountains to the sea...
While vessels in the harbor
Scurried to and fro,
Taking tourists to a sunset
Or, perhaps, to a whale watch show.

374

I felt as one with Nature
As I watched the palm trees sway,
Caressed by gentle Tradewinds
That among their fronds do play.

The cirrus clouds looked down on me
From the clear Lahaina skies,
In shapes of surfboards and of whales:
One surfboard just my size...

So when my friend, who had been shopping,
Returned from the banyan tree,
He found my suitcase, and my shoes,
But not a trace of ME.

About the Author

$\mathcal{C}$raig E. Burgess graduated from Audubon High School in Audubon, New Jersey, as the Valedictorian of the Class of 1963. He entered Rutgers University as a Pre-Med student, then changed his major after his sophomore year, graduating with a double major in languages: Spanish and German. He received a Teaching Fellowship at the University of Pennsylvania and, in 1968, was hired as a Spanish instructor for the new Cherry Hill High School EAST, located only six miles from his home in Audubon. Burgess completed his master's degree at Penn—in Education—in 1971 and spent his entire twenty-six-year teaching career at CHHSE, taking early retirement in 1994. While at EAST, he served as Language Department Chairperson for six years and as faculty advisor to the Spanish Honor Society, the school's Adopt-A-Grandparent program, and the International Literary Club—a group of students who received national recognition for its language magazine, *Passport.*

In 1993, Burgess was named the Individual Volunteer of the Year by the New Jersey Association of Healthcare Facilities (NJAHF) for his work with the Adopt-A-Grandparent program. In 1995, he and Mrs. Amy Maricondi, Activities Director at the then Meridian Nursing Home (now the Genesis Eldercare Complex), co-authored a book on Intergenerational Sharing and Caring: a handbook for AAG programs. In 1998, Burgess was awarded two Silver Bowls for excellence at the annual International Platform Association (IPA) convention in Washington, D.C.: one award for poetry, one for finishing first in the Speaking Ladder Competition. He then served as Facilitator for the Speaking Ladder Competition at the 1999 and 2000 IPA events. In 1999, he was named the Delegate of the Year by the International Biographical Centre (IBC) in Cambridge, England, at the International Congress on Arts & Communication Convention in Lisbon, Portugal. The same organization honored him in 2003 as an International Writer of the Year for his work in the areas of poetry and patriotism.

Burgess served as liaison to the U.S. Navy from the students in the Audubon High School Project Memorial Foundation from 1994 to 2014. From 1995 to 1999, he served as President of the Camden County Retired Educators' Association (CCREA), as President of the Audubon High School Alumni Association, and as a member of the Board of Directors for the Westmont Theatre Repertory Arts Group. Following his retirement from teaching in 1994, he also was active in the local Lions' Club for nearly fifteen years, became the town historian, gave presentations on poetry and patriotism in schools from New Jersey to Hawaii, and visited more than a dozen nursing homes and assisted living complexes in New Jersey each month, giving travel video presentations and visiting with the residents.

Burgess' writing "career" began in 1987—at the age of forty-two—after receiving national recognition for a poem he had composed on one of his forty-one visits to the Hawaiian Islands: a poem entitled "A Fleeting Glimpse of Paradise", the title selected for this collection of photographs and poems, a collection published after more than thirty years of experiences in the islands.

In 1995, Burgess founded a local organization of writers known as the Audubon Poets. Between 1995 and 2005, the group grew from three to more than forty members and published two anthologies of original verse: *The Best of the Audubon Poets in 1997; The Audubon Poets, Volume II, the Journey Continues,* in 2003. In addition to monthly reading sessions at the free public library in Audubon, members shared their work at a number of special programs and sponsored an annual poetry competition for young writers.

Having been inspired by the young patriotic students at his alma mater in Audubon, Burgess self-published a book on patriotism in 2000: a book dedicated to the students in the Project Memorial Foundation and focusing on a 1949 student who joined the Navy as a Corpsman, was killed in action in Korea on September 5, 1952, and is a recipient of the Medal of Honor (one of THREE individuals who lived and studied in Audubon and are recipients of the Medal of Honor). The book, *The Green Wave and the Navy: The History of the USS Benfold (DDG-65),* was made into a documentary film that was released in 2004.

The local veterans of American Legion Post #262 in Audubon honored Burgess for his patriotic efforts by designating September 9, 1999 "Craig E. Burgess Day" in the borough. In October of 2000, his alma mater selected him as one of the Charter members of the newly established Alumni Association's

"Ring of Honor". (Burgess was unable to attend the induction ceremony because he had taken seven students and several community leaders to New Orleans for the Christening of a second vessel to be named in memory of a Medal of Honor recipient from Audubon: the USNS *Brittin* (T-AKR 305). The naval supply vessel was named for Army Sergeant Nelson V. Brittin, a graduate of the AHS Class of 1939 who served in both World War II and in Korea and who was killed in action in Korea on March 7, 1951.

In 2010, having been diagnosed with a form of cancer and having started a year of chemotherapy, Burgess put together a chapbook entitled *Poetic Images of Cancer*, at the request of his hematologist, Dr. Howard I. Kesselheim, of the Regional Cancer Care Associates in Cherry Hill, New Jersey. The chapbook is in its sixth printing as of March of 2015, and Burgess has distributed more than twenty-seven hundred copies to cancer patients and to medical professionals who work with cancer patients. Now in remission from cancer, Burgess has been able to complete the special tribute to the Hawaiian Islands—the book you have just finished reading.

Sunset reflected at poolside at the Outrigger Napili Shores Resort on the island of Maui: May 1997